America Strong
O, House of Israel, Wake Up!

Wallace Stanciel

Published by So It Is Written, LLC

Detroit, MI

SoItIsWritten.net

Published by So It Is Written, LLC

Detroit, MI

SoItIsWritten.net

So It Is
Written

Copyright © 2024 by Wallace Stanciel

America Strong: O, House of Israel, Wake Up!

Edited by So It Is Written, www.SoItIsWritten.net

ISBN: 979-8-9888204-4-4

LCCN: 2024903040

Printed in the United States of America

TABLE OF CONTENTS

INTRODUCTION

W hen reading this book, I'm not trying to change anyone's mindset regarding what you believe or what you were taught based on religion preference. This book is the answer to my prayer, which I decided to share it with you: Heavenly Father, I got introduced to your Son at an incredibly early age and was told that his name is Jesus. So, I grew up believing this to be true: Heavenly Father, I'm seeking the truth from you, what is your Son true name? And I would like to know who I am according to your bloodline? So please, introduce me to myself and uncover me so I can see, where do I fit in according to your promise to Israel. And allow me to see what other people see when they see me, establish a relationship with me and introduce yourself to me like you did with Moses. This book is the answer from my prayer which I received from the Holy Spirit, to help me to establish a relationship with my God – YAHUAH. Have anyone ever wondered besides me; if Jesus came in his Father name then what is his Father name? Because the name of God or Heavenly Father is a title not a name! If we used the biblical timeline and go back in time, we will not find the name of Jesus as our Messiah. And what if I tell you that the name of Jesus wasn't at all seen in any English language literature until the 1700's, would you believe me?

1

Also what if I tell you that the name of Jesus is a Greek name not a Hebrew name but the name Iesous was found in the 1535 Coverdale Bible and in the 1560 Geneva Bible, however in 1611 King James Bible, we can find the name Iesus. Now, let's keep it real! Would Joseph and Mary – which their Hebrew name would had been, Yoceph for Joseph and Miryam for Mary also they both were in the bloodline descendants of King David: And a direct descendant of Avraham (Abraham), Yitschaq (Isaac) and Ya'aqov (Jacob).   Have we forgotten: When Yoceph (Joseph) receiving instruction from the angel concerning the name to be placed on the child.   In the Divine Book – Eth CEPHER (The Hebrew Bible), in Mattithtyahu (Mattew) 1:18-25 that say, "Now the birth of; Yahusha Ha'Mashiach (meaning: Salvation in the Messiah), was on this wise: When as his mother Miryam (Mary) was espoused to Yoceph (Joseph), before they come together, she was found with child of the Ruach Ha'Qodesh.   Then Yoceph (Joseph) her man, being just man, and not willing to make her a public example, was minded to put her away (privately).   But while he thought on these things, behold, the angel of Yahuah appeared unto him in a dream saying, Yoceph (Joseph) son of David, fear not to take unto you Miryam (Mary) your woman; for that which is conceived in her is of the Ruach Ha'Qodes.   And she shall bring forth a son, and you shall call his name – Yahusha, for he shall save his people (from) their sins.   Now all this was done, that it might be fulfilled which was spoken of Yahuah by the prophet, saying: Behold!

2

A virgin shall be with child, and shall bring forth a son, and they shall call the name of the same – Immanu'el: Which being interpreted is – our "El" is with me. Then Yoceph (Joseph) being raise from sleep did as the Angel of Yahuah, had bidden him and took unto him this woman. And knew her not till she had brought forth her firstborn son, and he called his name – Yahusha." According to the text, Yahuah first revealed himself to a Hebrew man named Abraham, who became known as the founder of Judaism. At that time the Jews believe that Yahuah made a special covenant with Abraham and that he and his descendants were chosen people who would create a great nation. Abraham's son Isaac and his grandson Jacob, also became the central figures in ancient Jewish history. Jacob took the name Israel, and his children and future generations became known as the Israelites. More than 1,000 years after Abraham, the prophet Moses, led the Israelites out of Egypt, after being enslaved for hundreds of years. According to scriptures, God revealed his laws known as the Ten Commandments, to Moses at Mt. Sinai. Around 1000 B.C., King David ruled the Jewish Nation: His son King Solomon built the first Holy Temple in Jerusalem, which became the central place of worship for the Jewish Nation. The Kingdom fell apart around 931 B.C., and the Jewish Nation, split into two Great Nation: Israel in the North and Judah in the South. Sometime around 587 B.C., the Babylonians, destroyed the first Holy Temple and sent many Hebrew speaking people that was the Jewish Nation into exile.

A second Holy Temple was built in 516 B.C., but was eventually destroyed by the Romans Empire in A.D. 70. The destruction of the second Holy Temple was significant to the Jewish Nation – Hebrew, could no longer gather or had a place to gather so they shifted their focus to worshiping in local synagogues but today we call these places – Church. I hope this book will make an intelligent conversation of "Who we are" and help with establishing a better relationship with your "El" - God, but allow the Ruach Ha'Qoesh - Holy Spirit to guide you on your journey seeking the truth also establish a personal relationship with your – Messiah: Yahusha, along the way. The NIV Quiet Time Bible, is the bible that I read from because it's easy to read and understand, without using a bible reference. Also I read the Book of Mormon, because it testify that the bible is true, and its main focus is this Beautiful Land called America. And the coming of the Messiah, therefore, the Bible and the Book of Mormon represents the Two Witnesses in America, both books talk about His coming, His birth and His ministry about Grace, His New Law and about His death, but the most important part is His resurrection. But what a lot of people forgot is his promise about the "The Coming Kingdom On Earth – the One Thousand Years Of Rest" before the second coming of the Messiah. However, the third important book that I read is called the ETH CEPHER, which means "The Divine Book: The Hebrew Bible, which have the Dead Sea Scrolls, the Apocrypha and the Bible all in one book. But what makes this book so special that it has the name of God, in it!

This is the reason why I don't use the name of Jesus, anymore, because of my journey searching for the truth. Along the way I discover that Jesus is a God, but a Greek God, and he is the Son of Zeus and some even call him - Zeus, which is not Hebrew. Therefore, believe me when I say this: I am not trying to disrespect anyone who believe in the name of Jesus, because I grew up worshiping this name, and taught my children about the important of this name. I'm not an atheist or anti-Christianity, it's all about having a relationship with the Holy Spirit, and allowing the Spirit of God, to help us to remember. According to the ETH CEPHER in Proverbs 30:4-9 "Who has ascended up into heaven, or descended? Who has gathered the wind in his fists? Who has bound the waters in a garment? Who has established all the ends of the earth? What is His name, and what is His Son's name, if you can tell? *(tell)*. Every word of ELOAH is pure: He is a shield unto them that put their trust in him. Add not unto his words, lest he reprove you, and you be found a liar. Two things have I required of you; deny me them not before I die: Remove far from me vanity and lies: Give me neither poverty nor riches; feed me with food convenient for me: Lest I be full, and deny you and say, who is YAHUAH? Or lest I be poor, and steal, and take the name of my ELOHIYM in vain." And Isaiah 42:8 "I am YAHUAH: That is my name; and my glory will I not give to another, neither my praise to graven images." As biblical understanding relates to African Americans, we lack understanding of our biblical timeline and why God kept his children in slavery throughout world history.

5

However, we have to remember nothing happens that is not planned or permitted by God: He is a God who orders all events according to his own will and future events to come. The translators of the Bible covered up and hide the real name of – YAHUAH, for a reason, and the most significant name in the Bible is – Hebrew. YAHUAH representing YAH – the name of He who visited Moses at the burning bush, and in the Hebrew language, we can find "VAV" creating the "SHUA or USHA" sound which is constructed to mean to make equal, therefore, the uniquely used name of YAHUSHA can be understood as YAH, which is the shortened name for YAHUAH. However, these two names are one, seeking the Kingdom of Heaven is seeking the name of Creator – HalleluYah – Praise-YAH. And we should establish a relationship with Him through His Son: But what does it mean when the translators say; they have adopted a device? It's a thing made or adapted for a particular purpose like a plan, a method or a trick aim to deceived for a particular purpose to change the name of the Almighty Creator, from YAHUAH to LORD, and from ELOHIYM to God, and from YAHUSHA to Jesus; so that no one can truly know their real name. Every one of us has a name, and it's very respectable for people to call other people by our proper name. According to the NIV Quiet Time Bible in Exodus 3:15 that says, "God also said to Moses: Say to the Israelites, the LORD, the God of your fathers – the God of Abraham, the God of Isaac and the God of Jacob – has sent me to you. This is my name forever, the name by which I am to be remembered from generation to generation."

And if we read this scripture out of the ETH CEPHER, it will give us the name that we should remember from generation to generation – which is: YAHUAH ELOHAI. But a device was adopted to cover up the name of the Almighty Creator, and yes, it was a scheme to hide the real name of YAHUAH. A day will come, and that day is now according to Isaiah 52:6 that says, "Therefore my people will know my name; therefore, on that day they will know that it is I who foretold it. Yes, it is I." And according to the NIV Quiet Time Bible in Acts 4:12 that says, "Salvation is found in no one else for there is no other name under heaven given to men by which we must be saved." Today we fail to understand or even imagine what our ancestors went through just to have the name of Jesus, forced on them, we went from Negro Christian Slaves to just Negro, then to Color, then to African American. And we are still holding on to a religion of hope embracing the name of Jesus as our Savior. According to John 4:24 that says, "God is a Spirit: and they that worship him must worship him in spirit and in truth." However, it's scripturally impossible for the name of Jesus to be used as our Savior because the letter "J" is less than five hundred years old. If we look into the 1611 King James Bible the translators used the name Iesus than change the name to Jesus by 1628, but in the Hebrew language this name mean "Horse" and in the Latin language the meaning is "Pig" however in the Greek language the name of Jesus means "Praise Zeus" which is a pagan deity with a birthday on December 25. And if you don't believe me; please check out http://www.hiddenbible.com.

7

Then click on the box, The Messiah vs. Zeus. Is Jesus, Zeus – Hidden Bible Home Page: What is the real name of the Messiah: Defaming the Messiah Iesous = Hail Zeus or Jesus = Hail Zeus." The name of Jesus is a 400-year-old name approximately, because the English language never had the letter "J" till then. Knowing information like this is extremely important because it says in the Bible by one name you shall be saved. So, it becomes frightfully important because the name of Jesus is not known by the Almighty Creator. On the other side of this subject, we are worshiping a Greek God, name – Zeus, who is a representation of the Sun God, who is known as the Devil, in the ancient cultures. This is a part of our Black Biblical History: Antiochus Epiphanes IV (Antiochus the Visible God – a Greek King), he was known as a madman the persecution of Jews in Judea, these was the ones who rebel and that started the Maccabees Revolt. They were under his jurisdiction and they suffer from the edits forbidding the Jewish people from observing their Holy Day - the Sabbath, and not allowing their newborn to be circumcised, than he place a statue of Zeus a supreme deity of the Greek Pantheon in the Jewish Temple in Jerusalem. And demanded similar statue in every Jewish town and village but the ultimate humiliation, when he build an altar in the Jewish Temple of God, to sacrifice pigs to the deity Zeus; it was this act that leaded to the Maccabean Revolt.

However, one of the greatest deceptions happened around 325 A.D. at Council Nicaea, the name of Jesus Christ was introduced to the world by Emperor Constantine and his church bishops with the purpose of eliminate other gods under the "Guises" an external form of an appearance, or a manner of presentation typically concealing the true nature of something. According to the NIV Quiet Time Bible in John 5:43 that say, "I have come in my Father's name and you do not accept me; but if someone else comes in his own name, you will accept him." I understand, when people say, because I don't speak Hebrew: This name doesn't matter, but it does!

9

What Hostility Are We Still Carrying

D o we really have a love-hate relationship with the will of God, versus our own will and desires? The Apostle Paul's letter to the church at Ephesus still stands today when we talk about faithfulness in the Messiah but how do we demonstrate faithfulness? First, by understanding there's other spiritual book's one particular called: The Eth CEPHER, which have the name of God in it, his Hebrew name that He introduce Himself to Moses by and in this book we will find the name YAHUHA – for the Father, the name YAHUSHA – for the Son and the name Ruach Ha'Qodesh – for the Holy Spirit. Therefore, according to the NIV Quiet Time Bible in Ephesians 1:1-14 that says, "Paul, an Apostle of Christ Jesus by the will of God, to the saints in Ephesus, the faithful in Christ Jesus: Grace and peace to you from God our Father and the Lord Jesus Christ. Praise be to the God and Father of our Lord Jesus Christ, who has blessed us in the heavenly realms with every spiritual blessing in Christ. For he chose us in him before the creation of the world, to be holy and blameless in his sight; in love he predestined us to be adopted as his sons through Christ. In accordance with his pleasure and will – to the praise of his glorious grace, which he has freely given us in the One he loves. In him we have redemption through his blood, the forgiveness of sins, in accordance with the riches of God's grace that he lavished on us with all wisdom and understanding.

And he made known to us the mystery of his will according to his good pleasure, which he purposed in Christ, to be put into effect when the times will have reached their fulfillment – to bring all things in heaven and on earth together under one head even Christ, when you heard the word of truth, the gospel of your salvation. Having believed, you were marked in him with a seal, the promised – the Holy Spirit. Who is a deposit guaranteeing our inheritance until the redemption of those who are God's possession – to the praise of his glory." HalleluYAH – Praise-YAH. Have we forgotten that all humanity belongs to the Messiah: And the family of Christ is a multi-ethnic community of people and families, so why are we still carrying hostility towards one of God family member, especially speaking of the LGBTQ2+ because they belong to God Family, just like everybody else who believes in his Son. He is no longer walking the earth healing people, but He still loves everyone: This is what Christ meant when He said: Come as you are! He is speaking to our spiritual state of mind. It has nothing to do with our gender, lifestyle, the way we dress, how much money we have, our living condition or our position in life. According to the NIV Quiet Time Bible in Matthew 11:27-30 that says, "All things have been committed to me by my Father: No one knows the Son, except the Father, and no one knows the Father, except the Son, and those to whom the Son chooses to reveal him. Come to me, all you who are weary and burdened, and I will give you rest. Take my yoke upon you and learn from me, for I am gentle and humble in heart, and you will find rest for your souls. For my yoke is easy and my burden is light."

And if we're not careful, the deceiver will mislead God's children to live a life of selfishness, with a title of born-again believer and having the spirit of evilness and full of vanity. The Bible are not merely historical chronicles they are narrative announcements that makes significant claim that Jesus Christ is the Messiah the High Priest of Israel and the Lord of the world. So the whole story of the gospel is introduce in Ephesians, in Christ we are blessed, we are chosen, predestined, redeemed, united, we have inheritance, we are sealed and by "Faith" we are save and the only way to overcome the evil spirit of this world we must put on the Armor of God, which represent – Love.   This is the Truthunedited.com – That modern day Judaism has made it; that the name of YAHUAH, was not to be used, said or called upon and basically have made it to be an curse to say the wounderful name of God. According to the Eth CEPHER in Exodus 20:7 that says, "You shall not take the name of YAHUAH ELOHAYKA in vain; for YAHUAH will not hold him guiltless that takes his name in vain."

Wake Up

Malcolm X once stated: "Sometimes a fruit falls from a tree, and rolls so far away from its roots, that it's no longer of the tree. The hard fall and long journey bruise the fruit, so much that it totally changes it! It's the same way for some of our people. This is why some can't be awakened regardless of how much truth you present to them. This journey has totally "Brainwashed" them to such a degree, that they're no longer of the original tree."

This book is going to shake some African American religious core values because it's also going to shake some of their belief system about: Christianity, and about the name of Jesus. Because this religious has control over God chosen people mind, if you believe in the Messiah, because He gives us access to our Father in Heaven. Please, don't reject the Heavenly Father, we are trying to come to Him and to be accepted by Him. However, Mr. Ronald Dalton Jr. is the author of a book called: Hebrew to Negroes – Wake up Black America. Purchase his book or watch part I and part II of his documentary; while he explained the transformation of a nation of people that went from Hebrew to Negroes. This is an exclusive interview of his belief and awakening that we are Hebrew's by bloodline, therefore watch this documentary.

Some African American, do not even know that our
ancestor were stripped of everything even their children and
forced to convert into this religious that is called:
Christianity, then led into slavery by the Spanish and
Portuguese Government, around the 1500's. First, our
ancestors were Messianic Judaism, which is different from
Christianity. They were descendants of the Twelve Tribes of
Israel, the Original Black Nation and they acknowledged:
Abraham, Isaac and Jacob as the Patriarchs of Israel, and
didn't acknowledge the name "Jesus" as their Messiah.
Christians are typically non-Jewish people, like in the Book
of Acts. It was the Apostle Paul, that made the way for the
Gentiles from Acts to Philemon. The Book of Acts forges a
new sense of identity and the disciples gradually realized
they were no longer Jews, at least from the confessional and
ceremonial points of view. The disciples slowly began to
understand that they were part of a new community of the
Holy Spirit, which was prophesied in the Hebrew Scriptures.
And the disciples seen the need to call all people Jews and
Gentiles, to repentance, and fellowship with this new
community and the church – baptism in the name of the
Father (YAHUAH), the Son (YAHUSHA), and the Holy
Spirit (RUACH HA'QODESH), also having communion
with the Lord's Supper became the outward signs of the
inward grace, with the emphasis on relationship to
experience a spiritual rebirth and reconciliation with God The
Father. But the ultimate question is: Why did our Black
spiritual leaders still practice - Christianity, especially when
we were given freedom back in 1865?

And why didn't our Black spiritual leaders return God's children back to our true religious? Was it because of the system we are under called "Imperialism" having an economic, exploratory, ethnocentric, political and religious gain, over the land and the people. African American, have a serious case of identity crisis and suffering from centuries of racial disparities, we didn't choose this religious, it got forced on our ancestors and we continued to take on this religion called: Christianity as a tradition from our former slave master, they use this religious to control our mind and mislead their slaves to obey them. To get an understanding of Imperialism by reading this book called: America - The New Imperialism; From White Settlement to World Hegemony. By: V. G. Kiernan with a preface by Eric Hobsbawm. The overview of this book is the invasion and occupation of Iraq, having sparked considerable discussion about the nature of American imperialism, but most of it's focused on the short term. The classical historical approach of this book provides a convincing and compelling analysis of the distinct phases of American imperialism, which have now led to America becoming a global hegemon without any serious rivals. Victor Kiernan, one of the world's most respected historians, has used his nuanced knowledge of history, literature and politics to trace the evolution of the American Empire: He includes accounts of relations between Indians and white settlers, readings of the work of Melville and Whitman, and an analysis of the way that money and politics became so closely intertwined.

Eric Hobsbawm's preface provides an insight into his own thoughts on American imperialism, and a valuable introduction to Victor Kiernan's work. Together, they shed useful light on today's urgent debates about the uses and misuses of seemingly unlimited money and military power; a lack of respect for international agreements, and the right to preemptive defense. Here in America, imperialism is the foundation that built this country; economic, exploratory, ethnocentric, political and religious gain, over the land and over the people but this is not a laughing matter because Black people have lost their identity when it comes down to religious. But we must come to the question of: What is hegemony? It's leadership or dominance, especially by one country or social group over others. In addition, the United States has also established institutional hegemony in the international economic and financial sector by manipulation the weighted voting systems, rules and arrangements of international organizations including approval by 85 percent majority and its domestic trade laws and regulation. Think about this, Dr. Claud Anderson stated: We are the only group people that came to this country that were enslaved, we were classified 3/5 of a human being and were classified as special property and the whole constitution was frame around legal rights and citizenship but not for black people, we were the only group of people that fought in every war, and the civil war was fought over – slavery. And we are the most patriotic group of people in this country beside white people, but still no reparation. Black people in this country have suffers from racial disparities for a long time say about 46 years up to the civil rights movement.

We are the only group of people that have been psychologically, emotionally, politically, educationally damaged and no one is trying to find out why our behavior is inappropriate. Where is our Black leaders? Who cares about the Black race? Oh, they all been assassinated! However now America, wants to pretend that we are all equal, but we are not, because by 1966 the white race had become economic giants, owning and controlling everything like wealth, privileges, resources, businesses and all levels of government. Everything that happen to Black people in this country was systematically programmed and still systematically programmed called: Social Engineering, an underclass structure to inappropriate behavior pattern for Black people here in America. Racism is a power structure that build a relationship with a group of people known as "Imperialism" meaning leadership or domination that one group of people have control over wealth, power and resources that can deprive, hurt, injury and exploit another group of people to provide for itself; So this exempt African-Americans because everything that black people have we get it from another group of people. Meaning that Black people control nothing! But how did this inappropriate behavior pattern got started here in America? It was around 1705, when the colonies pass slave codes to regulate their behavior, and what they must do to stay in line. So the colonies pass the Diversity Act – Virginia Slave Codes of 1705, formally entitled an act concerning servants and slaves, were a series of laws enacted by the Colony of Virginia's House of Burgesses, regulating the interactions between slaves and citizens of the crown colony of Virginia.

17

The enactment of the Slave Codes is considered to be the consolidation of slavery in Virginia and served as the foundation Virginia's slave legislation and all servants from non-Christian land that became slaves. There were forty-one parts of this code each defining a different part of the law surrounding the slavery in Virginia. The laws were devised to establish a greater level of control over the rising number of African slave population of Virginia and also socially segregated white colonists from Black enslaved persons, making them disparate groups (the start of – Racial Disparites) and hindering their ability to unite. Then in 1710 the Virginia Colonies passed a law call Meritorious Manumission, because the concept of Uncle Tom didn't just crop up out of thin air, some people point to the Meritorious Manumission Act, a law passed in Virginia back in the 1700's as the propellant that spurred Black people to snitch on one another to get into the good graces of white people. Under this law slaves could earn their freedom by performing good deeds that impressed their slave owners and some Black activists say, that this law not only caused Black people to turn on one other, but ultimately resulted in the creation of Black politicians who played along with the establishment instead of disrupting it. The act encouraged enslaved Africans to gain their personal freedom by keeping their masters informed on fellow enslaved Africans, who were planning and executing revolts and rebellions.

18

However this behavior has trickled down to the modern day and persists even today, therefore we still have some meritorious manumission Black leaders running around prioritize their personal ambition and rugged individualism over the liberation of the masses of our people from capitalism. In fact, the manumission mindset is so ingrained in the Black culture, and some experts said slave behavior will not disappear. A lot Black people don't know about or want to talk about Willie Lynch, speech known as "The Letter" – Called: The Making of the Slave. Some people said, he was from Jamaica, some people said, he was from Germany and some people said, that he was from India. But who cares; this is a must-read letter that every Black person should read. His speech was purportedly delivered to an audience on the bank of the James River in Virginia in 1712, regarding control of slaves within the colony but in recent years, it has been widely exposed as a hoax. However, this letter or short speech was given by a slave owner telling other slave owners that he discovered the secret to controlling Black slaves by setting them against one another. The document has been in print since 1970, but first gained widespread notice in the 1990s. When it appeared on the internet since then, it has often been promoted as an authentic account of slavery during the 18th century, though its inaccuracies and anachronism have led historians to conclude that it is a hoax, but ready, the speech credit the narrator's name as the source of the terms "lynching or the Lynch Law" therefore a man named William Lynch did indeed claim to have originated the term during the American Revolutionary War.

Other may say, the early use of the term "Lynch Law" came from Charles Lynch, a Virginia justice of the peace and militia officer during the American Revolution. After the slave owners heard William Lynch speech for social conditioning, controlling and brainwashing of the Black slaves: First, they had to physically control their slaves, second, created laws to have checks and balance legally over the slaves and third, it was "Symbolically" they had to make the slave think, that they are someone else "Christian" to establish control over them (Religion Gain) so they put a Bible together to control the mind of the slave to obey their master. The slave owners gave the Black slaves a religion not to help them, but to control them, and what Black people still have today is called: The same old religious that our slave master's taught the Blace race to control to control our mind locking us into slavery on a mental level. Now we have: Universities, Colleges and Institutions of Ministries again this is called: Imperialism. Black history is everywhere sometime we have to search for it, because it's hidden right in front of our face starting with the – Inquisition which occurred around the same time as the Transatlantic Slave Trade got started and by the same countries that took our ancestors identity away. This part of Black History is particularly important because it helps identify African American as Hebrew. Which is significant. The Edicts that came out of the Catholic Church, were a Declaration of Expulsion - that was issued by King John II, King John III and King Emmanuel of Spain.

This was nothing but a wrath from the devil, therefore to really get a description of who we are: We have to take trip back in world history, starting around the 1300's looking toward Spain and Portugal. And focus on the Palpable and the Edicts that was issued against the Black Jewish people and the Black Muslims people in this time period in history. We will discover our true identity, and it's this piece of black history that's not talked about because it will uncover our true identity as the real Nation of Israel. All throughout the Bible: God's people have a history on earth that led them into slavery repeatedly because of disobedience. Our God, is still waiting for His people to wake up, and discover the truth to who we are, and who we are not! In 1478 Pope Sixtus IV (21 July 1414 – 12 August 1484) was the head of the Catholic Church and ruler of the Papal States from 9 August 1471, to his death, however he founded the Spanish Inquisition allowing King Ferdinand and Queen Isabella of Spain to establish a special branch of the Inquisition, which led to an Anti-Semitic violence that expelled the Black Jewish people and Black Muslims people who were unwillingly to convert into "Christianity" by baptize. Some flee to Portugal while others were put on ships to be places on the West Banks of Africa, around 1500's. A book to reference this is called: The Rise of the Inquisition – An Introduction to the Spanish and Portuguese Inquisitions by Juan Marcos Bejarano Gutierrez. In this book you will discover about eight hundred thousand Black Jewish and Black Muslims people, that were expelled from Spain to the West Coast of Africa; because they were given an ultimatum to convert over to Roman Catholic Religion – Christianity.

21

Or get out the country, and some did decided to leave rather than convert over. When Christopher Columbus, arrived at the New World, he was a Christian bring Christianity with him and still today Christianity is the number one religion system in North America. What people are leaving out of Black history, is that King John II, King John III and King Emmanuel played a critical role in this Inquisition these three King's, held a ransom over the Black Jewish and Black Muslims people, head and inspire taking away their wealth so they could not paid their taxes, however instead of them going to jail. The government put an lien on their property! This was the system that led them into slavery, then the Spanish Government, took their children away from the ages of 3 to 10 baptized them into Christianity, deported the children to St. Thomas or the West Coast of Africa to be raised my White Christian families. This part of Black history is not talked about in Black schools or colleges, but the question is: Why not? And what makes this so sad, that it's not mentioned at all during Black History Month. We have the right to know about this important event on how a nation of people identity got erased. Maybe, this is why the United States of America, thinks they don't owe African Americans any reparation because the finger is not pointed at this country. Even though they participate in a wrongful act call slavery, but what about racial disparities what caused the mental illness on a nation of people?

Was this a crime against humanity? Plus, there are two other books we need to reference about out identity as a nation of people, that is called: Secret Jews – The Complex Identity of Crypto-Jews and Crypto-Judaism by: Frederic David Mocatta. And the The Porugal – The Inquisition, by: Frederic David Mocatta. These book's give a heartbreaking understanding of the Inquisition by King John II, also will mention one of the curses that God place on His people for being disobedience to his Law, Statue and Commandment. Spain and Portugal are guilty of the most heinous crimes history, while hiding behind the teaching of their God – Jesus Christ, which is a Catholic Religion. This Inquisition was the system that got slavery started around the world during fourteen and fifteen century. Because the Black Jewish and Black Muslims people, will not convert over to the Roman Catholic Religion, if this would happen today, we will call this genocide or proselytize an attempt to convert someone from one religion belief to another. Remember, these are our ancestors the Black Jewish and Black Muslims people, they were stripped of everything even their name, their religion and their children taken away to be transported to the West Coast of Africa. But where did the name "Negro" come from? It originated from the King of Spain, who wrote into law that the name "Jewish" be taken away from the Black Jewish people, so they became "Black Portuguese" and the word "Black" in Portuguese mean "Negro."

The dictionary has a definition of the word as a member of a dark-skinned group of people originally native of Africa, so in the sixteen century a law was passed stripping away their true identity and this was the name that follow the slaves to the New World – Negro Christian Slaves. The NIV Quiet Time Bible in Deuteronomy 28:32-50 that says, "Your sons and daughters will be given to another nation, and you will wear out your eyes watching for them day after day, powerless to lift a hand. A people that you do not know will eat what your land and labor produce, and you will have nothing but cruel oppression all your days. The sights you see will drive you mad: God the Father will afflict your knees and legs with painful boils that cannot be cured, spreading from the soles of your feet to the top of your head. God the Father will drive you and the king you set over you to a nation unknown to you or your fathers. There you will worship other gods, gods of wood and stone. You will become a thing of horror and an object of scorn and ridicule to all the nations where God the Father, will drive you. You will plant much seed in the field, but you will harvest little, because locusts will devour it. You will plant vineyards and cultivate them, but you will not drink the wine or gather the grapes, because worms will eat them. You will have olive trees throughout your country, but you will not use the oil, because the olives will drop off. You will have sons and daughters, but you will not keep them, because they will go into captivity. Swarms of locusts will take over all your trees and the crops of your land. The alien who lives among you will rise above you higher and higher, but you will sink lower and lower.

He will lend it to you, but you will not lend it to him. He will be the head, but you will be the tail. All these curses will come upon you. They will pursue you and overtake you until you are destroyed, because you did not obey your God and observe the commands and decrees that he gave you. They will be a sign and a wonder to you and your descendants forever. Because you did not serve your God's joyfully and gladly in the time of prosperity, therefore in hunger and thirst, in nakedness and dire poverty, you will serve the enemies that God's send against you. He will put an iron yoke on your neck until he has destroyed you. God will bring a nation against you from far away, from the ends of the earth, like and eagle swooping down, a nation whose language you will not understand a fierce-looking nation without respect for the old or pity or the young." The 1490's mark the beginning of the Transatlantic Slave Transporting: The Negro Christian Slaves, but some scholars may say around the 1300's however Spain had a precedent for slavery as an institution since time of the Roman Empire. Also slavery existed among Native Americans of both Meso-America and South America, however the Monarch – the Spanish Crown attempted to limit the bondage of indigenous people because they rejected slavery based on race along therefore the Monarch gave grants to the colonist in the New World. This was called: The Conferring the Right of Demand Tribute and forced labor on the native inhabitant of any area, formally, the indigenous people held in encomienda that they were not slaves.

Soon after Christopher Columbus, returned from his first voyage to the new world it became apparent by the old world investors and Spanish Monarch, to realize that the New World possessed potential of a different sort "Plantation System and Refining Industry" this help shape the New World, with new economy and a new society with the help of institution of slavery. Although sugar cane plantation was the first planted in Brazil, around the 1500's, this was apparently done in the New World, for economic reasons. Africa became the Island of Perdition, or the Island of Punishment for the slaves, so why do we want to call ourselves African American? But first let's get an understanding of these two important questions: Why did God created time and why did God give human being so much time to repent? We can start off by saying that God gives perspective to our lives so we will have time to get to know Him and His Son. God wants His people to repent, so we can have a chance to highlights the forethought of His plan for redemption, and to give every human being a chance to enriches the context of the Gospel of Grace, also to verifies the inspiration of His plan to be true. Allowing mankind to helps establish environmental plan and culture on the earth, and to have an chance to get to know about "God Coming Kingdom" that's going to be on earth. Therefore, why created time at all so He can reveal that He is God of organization and structure, to highlights spiritual truths by measuring time itself, with critical memorials and displayed His signs. But, first, let's get an understanding of these two important questions: Why did God create time? Why did God give human beings so much time to our lives? It's so that we will have time to get to know Him and His Son.

According to the NIV Quiet Time Bible in Genesis 1:14-19 that says, "And God said, Let there be lights in the expanse of the sky to separate the day from the night and let them serve as signs to mark seasons and days and years and let them be lights in the expanse of the sky to give light on the earth. And it was so: God made two great lights – the greater light of govern the day and the lesser light to govern the night. He also made the stars. God set them in the expanse of the sky to give light on the earth, to govern the day and the night and to separate light from darkness. And God saw that it was good and there was evening, and there was morning – this mark the fourth day of creation." Which marks the beginning of "Time" along with the day, night and the season. Also, God didn't change his Sabbath! Exodus 20:8-11 that says, "Remember the Sabbath day by keeping it holy. Six days you shall labor and do all your work, but the seventh day is a Sabbath to the LORD your God. On it you shall not do any work, neither you nor your son or daughter, nor you manservant or maidservant, nor your animals, nor the alien within your gates. For in six days the LORD made the heavens and the earth, the sea and all that is in them, but he rested on the seventh day. Therefore, the LORD blessed the Sabbath day and made in holy." However it was the Angel of the LORD, that taught Moses how to track time starting with the day of creation, but we cannot forget the Gregorian timeline the original calendar so our starting point can be the Book of Genesis.

According to the NIV Quiet Time Bible in Genesis 5:3-5 that says, "When Adam has lived 130 years, he has a son in his own likeness, in his own image and he named him Seth. After Seth was born, Adam lived eight hundred years and had other sons and daughters, altogether, Adam lived 930 years, and then he died." Now in Genesis 5:6-32 that says, "When Seth had lived 105 years, he became the father Enosh. And after he became the father Enosh, Seth lived 807 years and had other sons and daughters, altogether, Seth lived 912 years and then he died. When Enosh had lived 90 years, he became the father of Kenan. And after he became the father of Kenan: Enosh lived 815 years and had other sons and daughters. Altogether, Enosh lived 905 years, and then he died. When Kenan had lived 70 years, he became the father of Mahalalel. And after he became the father of Mahalalel, Kenan lived 840 years and had other sons and daughters, altogether, Kenan lived 910 years, and then he died. When Mahalalel had lived 65 years, he became the father of Jared. And after he became the father of Jared, Mahalalel lived 830 years and had other sons and daughters. Altogether, Mahalalel lived 895 years, and then he died. When Jared had lived 162 years, he became the father of Enoch. And after he became the father of Enoch, Jared lived eight hundred years and had other sons and daughters. Altogether, Jared lived 962 years, and then he died. When Enoch had lived 65 years, he became the father of Methuselah and after he became the father of Methuselah. Enoch walked with God, for 300 years and had other sons and daughters.

Altogether, Enoch lived 365 years, then he was no more because God took him away. When Methuselah had lived 187 years, he became the father of Lamech. And after he became the father of Lamech, Methuselah lived 782 years and had other sons and daughters, altogether, Methuselah lived 969 years, and then he died. When Lamech had lived 182 years, he had a son. He names him Noah and said, "He will comfort us in the labor and painful toil of our hands caused by the ground the LORD has cursed." After Noah was born, Lamech lived 595 years and had other sons and daughters, altogether, Lamech lived 777 years, and then he died. After Noah was five hundred years old, he became the father of Shem, Ham and Japheth." Japheth was the oldest and the year of the flood was about 1656 years after time began, so this mean that Noah was born 1056 years after creation but remember that Moses is recording all of this from the angel of the LORD, who wrote the first five books of the bible. Now understand this; the timeline of the Patriarchy was about 2,300 hundred years or more, meaning more time had passed between Adam and Joseph than between Jesus, time on earth and today time. And these are the Books of History from Genesis to Esther, the years of Wisdom Literature is from Job to the Song of Solomon, the Major Prophets is from Isaiah to Daniel and to close out the Old Testament is the Minor Prophets from Hosea to Malachi. But when we turn the page to the New Testament another four hundred years passed.

But according to the NIV Quiet Time Bible in 2 Thessalonians 1:5-10 that says, "All this is evidence that God's judgment is right, and as a result you will be counted worthy of the Kingdom of God, for which you are suffering. God is just: He will pay back trouble to those who trouble you and give relief to you who are troubled, and to us as well. This will happen when the Lord Jesus in revealed from heaven in blazing fire with his powerful angels. He will punish those who do not know God and do not obey the gospel of our Lord Jesus. They will be punished with everlasting destruction and shut out from the presence of the Lord and from the majesty of his power on the day he comes to be glorified in his holy people and to be marveled at among all those who have believed. This included you because you believed our testimony to you." One of Christ follower Peter asserts that Christ was delivered up according to the definite plan and foreknowledge of God. According to the NIV Quiet Time Bible in Acts 2:23 that says, "This man was handed over to you by God's set purpose and foreknowledge; and you, with the help of wicked men, put him to death by nailing him to the cross." This was the God of Abraham, the God of Isaac, the God of Jacob and the God of our fathers – the prophets which glorified his Word: Even Paul, one of Christ follower argues that all who believe in Jesus Christ, regardless of their ethnicity or gender, inherit the blessing that God promised to Abraham.

According to the NIV Quiet Time Bible in Galatians 3:1-9 that say, "You foolish Galatians! Who has bewitched you? Before your very eyes Jesus Christ was clearly portrayed as crucified. I would like to learn just one thing from you: Did you receive the Spirit by observing the law, or by believing what you heard? Are you so foolish? After beginning with the Spirit, are you now trying to attain your goal by human effort? Have you suffered so much for nothing – if it really was for nothing? Does God give you his Spirit and work miracles among you because you observe the law, or because you believe what you heard? Consider Abraham: He believed God, and it was credited to him as righteousness. Understand, then, that those who believe are children of Abraham. The Scripture foresaw that God would justify the Gentiles by faith and announced the gospel in advance to Abraham: All nations will be blessed through you. So those who have faith are blessed along with Abraham, the man of faith."

Spiritual Sacrifice

Laws, Statutes, Judgment and Commandments
The Fundamentals of Spiritual Knowledge
&
The Keys to the Kingdom of God

Many believers don't understand that we are under the Seventh Covenant, better known as the New Covenant or the New Law. We have exclusive access to God and privileges to enjoy Him through His-Son our Messiah; also we are expected to offer up spiritual sacrifices. But not all sacrifices are accepted by God, because He is the same as yesterday, today and forever according to Hebrews 13:8. Therefore, one thing is clear throughout the Bible, obedience is better than sacrifice, because sacrifice without obedience is routine and at worst is abomination. The NIV Quiet Time Bible; says in Isaiah 1:1-3 that says, "The vision concerning Judah and Jerusalem that Isaiah's son of Amoz saw during the reigns of Uzziah, Jotham, Ahaz and Hezekiah, Kings of Judah. Hear, O heavens! Listen, O earth! For the LORD has spoken: I reared children and brought them up, but they have rebelled against me. The ox knows his master, the donkey his owner's manger, but Israel does not know, my people do not understand."

Overall, the Southern Kingdom had about twenty kings but only one stood out, that was King Josias, according to Ecclesiasticus 49:2-3 that says, "He behaved himself uprightly in the conversion of the people and took away the abominations of iniquity. He directed his heart unto the LORD, and in the time of the ungodly, he established the worship of God." The Sixth Covenant of Moses is highlighted in Numbers 28:1-31 – talks about tithing, and it has nothing to do with money, the true worshiping is how we come before the outer and inner court of the tabernacle: Which is our body, this is where the Holy Spirit dwells. We are to self-govern our body for true daily worshiping, this is one of the reasons why the Lord's Prayer, is important to start off our day it's our sin offering and trespass offering. And we suppose to pray this prayer to start off our day, which represents our daily spiritual sacrifice. However churches today don't offer a sin offering or a trespass offering that reigned from Adam to Moses; that stopped sin right in its tracks, but the pastor's just wanted their congregation to offer a sacrifice of money making them think that making a monetary gesture to God, is the only way to be forgiven of sin and trespass, therefore, the churches is no longer offering "Oblations" to chase away evil spirits. The NIV Quiet Time Bible says in Daniel 8:13-17 that says, "Then I heard a holy one speaking and another holy one said to him: How long will it take for the vision to be fulfilled – the vision concerning the daily sacrifice, the rebellion that causes desolation and the surrender of the sanctuary and of the host that will be trampled underfoot?

33

He said to me, it will take 2,300 evenings and mornings then the sanctuary will be re-consecrated. While I, Daniel, was watching the vision and trying to understand it, there before me stood one who looked like a man. And I heard a man's voice from the Ulai (The River or The Crystal Sea), calling Gabriel; tell this man the meaning of the vision. As he came near the place where I was standing, I was terrified and fell prostrate: Son of man, he said to me, understand that the vision concerns the time of the end." Daniel 8:19-27 that says, "He said: I am going to tell you what will happen later in the time of wrath, because the vision concerns the appointed time of the end. The two-horned ram that you saw represents the kings of Media and Persia. The shaggy goat is the king of Greece, and the large horn between his eyes is the first king. The four horns that replaced the one that was broken off represent four kingdoms that will emerge from his nation but will not have the same power. In the latter part of their reign, when rebels have become completely wicked, a stern-faced king, a master of intrigue, will arise. He will become very strong, but not by his own power. He will cause astounding devastation and will succeed in whatever he does. He will destroy the mighty men and the holy people. He will cause deceit to prosper, and he will consider himself superior. When they feel secure, he will destroy many and take his stand against the Prince of Princes. Yet he will be destroyed, but not by human power. The vision of the evenings and mornings that has been given you is true but seal up the vision for it concerns the distant future. I, Daniel, was exhausted and lay ill for several days.

Then I got up and went about the king's business. I was appalled by the vision; it was beyond understanding." From the fall of Adam, mankind was cursed for seven thousand years, and all the prophets from Joel to the Messiah; were counting down the 2,300 days or the 2,300 years until the 1,000 years of rest and the temple will be clean, so God's children will have their daily sacrifice. The High Priest, the Prince of Peace, the Son of God, will be our Messiah. Remember from the fall of the Persian Empire to the Messiah's death, it was about three hundred years and from his death, to the great rest or the Sabbatical Rest that is prophesied to come, will be about 2,000 years. This is where we get 2,300 years but the third temple has not been built and this is a mystery in our time: When will the third temple be built? Who knows! According to Daniel 12:4 in the NIV Quit Time Bible, the angel told Daniel to seal up this knowledge until the last day. "But you, Daniel, close up and seal the words of the scroll until the time of the end. Many will go here and there to increase knowledge." It is the Holy Spirit that's teaching God's children all things and brings the Word of God, back to our remembrance: According to 2 Chronicles 13:10-12 that says, "As for us, the LORD is our God, and we have not forsaken him. The priests who serve the LORD are sons of Aaron and the Levites assist them. Every morning and evening they present burnt offerings and fragrant incense to the LORD. They set out the bread on the ceremonially clean table and light the lamps on the gold lampstand every evening. We are observing the requirements of the LORD our God. But you have forsaken him.

God is with us: He is our leader. His priests with their trumpets will sound the battle cry against you. Men of Israel do not fight against the LORD, the God of our fathers, for you will not succeed." Those of us who consider themselves African Americans are so mentally messed up because we don't even know who we are! As it pertains to Black Biblical World History: The NIV Quiet Time Bible says in Isaiah 1:4-16 "Ah, sinful nation a people loaded with guilt a brood of evildoers, children given to corruption! They have forsaken the LORD; they have spurned the Holy One of Israel, and turned their backs on him. Why should you be beaten anymore? Why do you persist in rebellion? Your whole head is injured, your whole heart afflicted. From the sole of your foot to the top of your head there is no soundness, only wounds and welts and open sores, not cleansed or bandaged or soothed with oil. Your country is desolate your cities burned with fire, your fields are being stripped by foreigners right before you, laid waste as when overthrown by strangers. The Daughter of Zion is left like a shelter in a vineyard, like a hut in a field of melons, like a city under siege. Unless the LORD Almighty had left us some survivors, we would have become like Sodom, we would have been like Gomorrah. Hear the word of the LORD, you rulers of Sodom; listen to the law of our God, you people of Gomorrah! The multitude of your sacrifices – what are they to me? Says the LORD! I have more than enough of burnt offerings, of rams and the fat of fattened animals, I have no pleasure in the blood of bulls, lambs, and goats.

When you come to appear before me, who has asked this of you, this trampling of my courts? Stop bringing meaningless offerings! Your incense is detestable to me. New Moons, Sabbaths and convocations – I cannot bear your evil assemblies. Your New Moons festivals and your appointed feasts my soul hates. They have become a burden to me; I am weary of bearing them. When you spread out your hands in prayer, even if you offer many prayers, I will not listen. Your hands are full of blood; wash and make yourselves clean. Take your evil deeds out of my sight! Stop doing wrong, learn to do right! Seek justice, encourage the oppressed. Defend the cause of the fatherless, plead the case of the widow." The NIV Quiet Time Bible says in Deuteronomy 32:28 "They are a nation without sense there is no discernment in them, if only they were wise and would understand this and discern what their end will be!" We have forgotten about the oblations, sacrifices and our New Covenant or New Law, because some people are so busy telling other people that we are no longer under the Old Covenant or Old Law – everything that pertains to our greatness is in the Law of God. We are void of these things therefore we know extraordinarily little of what caused our set-back in Black Biblical World History. It was King Manasseh, who set up an abomination inside the Temple of God; that made the children of Israel desolate. Let's take the Christmas tree for example: It's an idol with a false God that brings presents and we have no problem lying to our children about this god, and we're still worshiping this idol in our today sanctuary of God.

37

In the Book of Jeremiah 31:31-34 that says, "The time is coming, declares the LORD, when I will make a New Covenant with the House of Israel, and with the House of Judah. It will not be like the covenant, I made with their forefathers when I took them by the hand to lead them out of Egypt, because they broke my covenant though I was a husband to them, declares the LORD. This is the covenant I will make with the House of Israel after that time, declares the LORD. I will put my law in their minds and write it in their hearts. I will be their God, and they will be my people. No longer will a man teach his neighbor, or a man his brother saying, know the LORD; because they will all know me from the least of them to the greatest, declares the LORD. For I will forgive their wickedness and will remember their sins no more." What a lot of people don't realize is that the statue of King Nebuchadnezzar is a biblical time clock or a calendar staring with King Nebuchadnezzar Kingdom, then the Media and Persians, the Greeks, then came the Romans. Now, we are dealing with the two feet that represent two powerful nation looking over the ten toes making this point in our time significant in world history. The NIV Quiet Time Bible says in Hebrews 8:1-2 "The point of what we are saying is this: We do have such a high priest, who sat down at the right hand of the throne of the Majesty in heaven, and who serves in the sanctuary, the true tabernacle set up by the LORD, not by man." And according to Malachi 3:6-12 that says, "I the LORD do not change. So, you, O descendants of Jacob, are not destroyed.

Ever since the time of your forefathers you have turned away from my decrees and have not kept them. Return to me, and I will return to you, says the LORD Almighty. But you ask; how are we to return? Will a man rob God? Yet you rob me. But you ask; how do we rob you? In tithes and offerings. Tithing is represented by keeping God's Commandment in Matthew 19:16-19, because we're to tithe to the Heavenly Father: He is our Creator. Offering is represented by the Second Greatest Commandment – Love or Respect your neighbor – in other words don't be afraid to help one another by offering a helping hand. You are under a curse – the whole nation of you – because you are robbing me. Bring the whole tithe into the storehouse, so that there may be food in my house. Test me in this, says the LORD Almighty, and see if I will not throw open the floodgates of heaven and pour out so much blessing that you will not have room enough for it. I will prevent pests from devouring your crops, and the vines in your fields will not cast their fruit, says the LORD Almighty. Then all the nations will call you blessed, for yours will be a delightful land, says the LORD Almighty." In this scripture God is talking about the order of obedience to His Commandment: Not money! He is talking about, Matthew 19:16-19 which is the keys to the kingdom, and our daily and evening sacrifices; is the Lord's Prayer and the meat offering; the drinking of wine and breaking of bread that represent our Messiah's body and his blood also all of his commandment's is tied in the oblations to chase evil spirits away.

This is important to be repeated: Tithes is not monetary! But how is this; because we have a New Covenant, which is our New Law and there is no mention of tithing and offerings of money in the New Testament. The final reason we know we're not commanded to give tithes or any percent of money, is because it's not commanded, or even recommended in the New Testament. The word tithe appears at least three times in the New Testament, starting with Matthew 23:23 that says, "Woe to you, teachers of the law and Pharisees, you hypocrites! You give a tenth of your spices – mint, dill and cumin. But you have neglected the more important matters of the law – justice, mercy and faithfulness. You should have practiced the latter, without neglecting the former." And Luke 11:42 that says, "Woe to you Pharisees, because you give God a tenth of your mint, rue and all other kinds of garden herbs, but you neglect justice and the love of God. You should have practiced the latter without leaving the former undone." And in Hebrews 7:5-17 that says, "Now the law requires the descendants of Levi who become priests to collect a tenth from the people – that is, their brothers – even though their brothers are descended from Abraham. This man, however, did not trace his descent from Levi, yet he collected a tenth from Abraham and blessed him who had the promises. And without doubt the lesser person is blessed by the greater. In the one case, the tenth is collected by men who die; but in the other case, by him who is declared to be living. One might even say that Levi, who collects the tenth, paid the tenth through Abraham, because when (King) Melchizedek met Abraham, Levi was still in the body of his ancestor.

If perfection could have been attained through the Levitical priesthood, for on the basis of it the law was given to the people, why was there still need for another priest to come – one in the order of (King) Melchizedek, not in the order of Aaron? For when there is a change of the priesthood, there must also be a change of the law. He of whom these things are said belonged to a different tribe, and no one from that tribe has ever served at the altar. For it is clear that our Lord descended from Judah, and in regard to that tribe, Moses said nothing about priests. And what we have said is even more clear if another priest like (King) Melchizedek appears, one who has become a priest not on the basis of a regulation as to his ancestry but on the basis of the power of an indestructible life. For it is declared: You are a priest forever, in the order of (King) Melchizedek." And this is the reason we do not have to give an offering or tithes because an offering has been given on the cross! Understand this; God gave his people the Levitical Law – which is sacrificial, He gave us Statutes to govern ourselves in an orderly way, but it was the Messiah who brought forth the New Law or the New Covenant – which He sprinkled and consecrated with his blood on the mercy seat – the Ark of the Covenant. Therefore, it is the Son of God who able to save completely those who come to the Father, through Him and it is the Spirit of God, who reminds us of the Gospel of Grace – God Word and His Spirit is always ready to intercede for Him. So we do not have offer up sacrifices day after day because our Messiah, sacrificed for all of our sins once and for all.

41

Wallace Stanciel

According to the NIV Quiet Time Bible in Hebrews 7:26-28 that says "Such a high pries meets our need – one who is holy, blameless, pure, set apart from sinners exalted above the heavens. Unlike the other high priest, he does not need to offer sacrifices day after day, first for his own sins, and then for the sins of the people. He sacrificed for their sins once and for all when he offered himself. For the law appoints as high priests men who are weak but the oath, which came after the law appointed the Son, who has been made perfect forever." There's a lot of un-answer questions about God and His Creation; but the only way to get some of these questions answer is to ask God himself. However we have to go through His Son, first, and if He choose to reveal them it's only my His grace and mercy. The NIV Quiet Time Bible in 2 Peter 3:8 that says, "But do not forget this one thing, dear friends: With the Lord a day is like a thousand years, and a thousand years are like a day." On this view, God's time does not map onto our time at all. His time is completely distinct from ours. Another view is that God is "Omnitemporal Being" meaning that God would be above physical time, but still temporally present, and thus able to enter into relations with temporal entities and it's true on this view, as well that God is in our time, but He experiences temporal succession in His being. Our time is constituted by physical time. God's time is "Metaphysical Time" has no intrinsic metric and is constituted purely by the "Divine Life" itself!

And if God is omnitemporal, His metaphysical time does map in some way into our physical time (Padgett 1992, 2001; DeWeese 2002, 2004). And is this how God knows everything? Another view (Craig, 2001a, 2001b) is that God became temporal when time was created. God's did existence without creation it was a timeless existence, but once temporal reality comes into existence, God himself must change. On this view, there was not a time when he was timeless because God's timelessness without creation is precisely due to the fact that time came into existence with creation. Now, answer this question? What is the Messiah 2030 – The Prophetic Messiah Timeline and is it true? There's a YouTube documentary on this subject – The Creation Prophecy: Please watch! However, what is the 7,000 years dispensational timeline? Some scholars predict it is from the original sin around 3971 B.C., which was the fall of Adam, then the timeline got reset, from the birth and death of the Messiah. Which took at least 4,000 years that reset time around 30 A.D. Now just making a wild guess; this means at least 2,000 years passed on the dispensational timeline since the Messiah death, which put us around 2024, right or wrong let's keep moving! This question is to all the scholars: Are we at the beginning of the seven years tribulation period? And is the Great Gathering Of The Lawlessness about to occur? Which may occur around 2030 or 2031; meaning the Messiah believer that's dead and live are going to spend one thousand years with the Messiah? Before his second coming in 3030 or 3031?

We know that no one knows the time or day when the trumpet will sound, therefore, how can we get an understanding of the theory of the 7,000 years dispensational timeline? Because we know that there's nothing new under the sun and all things will be revealed at the appointed time of what, where, and when is the finished work of the Messiah. The forty years disciplinary time-out for Judah's iniquity is about up, and according to the NIV Quiet Time Bible in the Book of Ezekiel Chapter 4 and 5 – Is The Warning the People of God. Some may argue that this prophecy was fulfilled in the first century when the temple was destroyed in 70 A.D., because it took forty years plus thirty more years to equals seventy years, but the secret and the mystery to unlocks this biblical timeline from the beginning to the end are revealed in the biblical calendar that was disclosed at least four times: The first in the NIV Quiet Time Bible that said; in Leviticus 26:18 that says, "If after all this you will not listen to me, I will punish you for your sins seven times over." The second in Leviticus 26:21 says: "If you remain hostile toward me and refuse to listen to me, I will multiply your afflictions seven times over, as your sins deserve." The third in Leviticus 26:24 that says: "I myself will be hostile toward you, and will afflict you for your sins seven times over." And the fourth in Leviticus 26:28 that says: "Then in my anger I will be hostile toward you, and I myself will punish you for your sins seven times over."

Despite all these pleadings from God, to the real Nation of Israel, to repent for being disobedience to His law because they lost their faith and became blind to the truth with unbelieving hearts which led them in murdering the Messiah, by one of the cruelest methods ever designed by mankind. Luke 23:20-21 that says, "Wanting to release Jesus, Pilate appealed to them again. But they kept shouting: Crucify him! Crucify him!" Now, let's do the math! If we start at 40 A.D., and multiply by seven, that will equal 280 A.D. Then if we take 280 A.D. + 70 A.D., this will bring us to the fourth century. Which will equal 350 A.D., and still the House of Israel did not repent, now, if we multiply 7 to 280 years, this will equal to 1960 years, then subtract 280 years for time served, which will give us 1680 years. Again, God promised 7 years multiplied to every period He allows for repentance but when there was no repentance, God declared that He would bring unrepentant Israel back into the land in a condition of unbelief and He did this on May 14, 1948. So, if we take 350 A.D. + 1680, it will equal 2030 A.D. Or if we take 70 A.D. + 280 years + 1680 years, we will still get 2030 A.D. Even if we take 70 A.D. + 1960 years, we will still get 2030 A.D. And what does this mean: The Prophecy of Jacob Trouble is about to end! God gave the House of Israel 7 x 7 years to belief and to repent which equal 49 years and if we take 1960 years divided by 49 years, it will equal 40 years of the Jubilee Cycles. So, if we take 49 years which was the time given and multiplied this by 40 years of the Jubilee Cycles, we will get 1960 years: So, if we take 70 A.D. + 1960 years + 1 year for the Jubilee Cycles, we will get 2031 A.D., for a Jubilee year.

Now, for the ultimate question: Does this mark the time for the Great Gathering Of The Lawlessness? For the House of Judah, the House of Israel, and for the Gentiles. And what is the long promised of the Rest Prophesies? Six days of labor equal six years, followed by one day of rest equal to one thousand years, with our Messiah. And if we continue to do the math all the way up to Adam, the first sin that brought a curse upon God Creation, around 3971 B.C., minus six thousand years, we will get 2029. Let's go back to the Book of Ezekiel Ch. 4 and 5 starting at 4:4-6, in the NIV Quiet Time Bible says, "Then lie on your left side and put the sin of the House of Israel upon yourself: You are to bear their sin for the number of days you lie on your side. I have assigned you the same number of days as the years of their sin. So, for 390 days you will bear the sin of the House of Israel. After you have finished this, lie down again, this time on your right side, and bear the sin of the House of Judah. I have assigned you 40 days, a day for each year." Therefore, how can we identify the two houses? The House of Israel is the Northern Kingdom of the land and what is their sign? The siege of Jerusalem by a foreign army and how long is the period of their iniquity, it's 390 days a year for each day: When did the time-out for repentance begin? In 701 B.C., when the Assyrians lay siege to Jerusalem, but God put a wall of iron around the city. Now Ezekiel, laid on his right side, for the House of Judah. Who is the House of Judah, the Southern Kingdom of the land and what is their sign? The siege of Jerusalem by a foreign army and how long is the period of iniquity for forty days a day for a year, and when did the time-out for repentance begin? 70 A.D.

So, this makes 770 years or 771 years apart! Now, if we multiply 390 x 7, we will get 2730 years subtract 701 B.C., we will get 2029, then added one year for the Jubilee Cycle, it will equal to 2030 A.D. The question we can all asked ourselves: Is God about to show His hand and proved to the world that He is in charge by uniting both Houses Israel and Judah. The unrepentant and unbelieving children of God, still have a chance to repent and believe in their Messiah, and live with Him, for one thousand years before He renew the earth and the heavens. But what is sad and frightful that a large remnant of God children will be cast with everlasting punishment. However, the Prophecy of Zechariah said only one third of the Lawlessness, are going to enter into the Sabbath Rest of Jubilee Cycle, this may happen around 2030 or 2031 A.D. Again, no one knows the day or the hour of the Great Gathering Of God's children, which will start the 7,000 years of the dispensation: Maranatha – Come, O LORD. According to the NIV Quiet Time Bible in 1 Corinthians 16:22 that says "If anyone does not love the Lord – a curse be on him. Come, O Lord!" These are two questions that should be answered! Does Christianity stop Black people from getting to know their true God? Is Christianity a weapon of mass destruction destroying the mind of God's children? The same God that Moses talked to, and the same God of Abraham, Isaac and Jacob: One more important question! Knowing the history of Christianity: Was this religious apart of White supremacy that's keeping Black people brainwashed in order to worship a White god?

By giving us a picture of him to worship, because this religious came from the Roman Empire, the same empire that murdered the Messiah. According to the NIV Quiet Time Bible in Revelation 12:9 that says, "The great dragon was hurled down – that ancient serpent called the devil, or Satan, who leads the whole world astray. He was hurled to the earth, and his angels with him." We can become blind to the Word of God, only because His people don't study His word properly for understanding, and this is how the spirit of devil can easily portray to be pastor or a minister misleading God children to give monetary offering for tithes, where it's nowhere in the New Testament, that our Messiah commanded for the children of God, to give a tenth of their earnings. But there are principles when it comes down to giving, according to 1 Corinthians 10:26 in the NIV Quiet Time Bible that says: "The earth is the Lord's, and everything in it." We are to manage our life and our money the best way as possible so His blessings and generosity are not wasted however, gaining money is only possible through God, so which spirit are we worshiping? Therefore, we should show gratitude by returning a portion back to God: According to 1 Timothy 6:17-19 that says, "Command those who are rich in this present world, not to be arrogant nor to put their hope in wealth, which is so uncertain, but to put their hope in God, who richly provides us with everything for our enjoyment. Command them to do good, to be rich in good deeds, and to be generous and willing to share. In this way they will lay up treasure for themselves as a firm foundation for the coming age, so that they may take hold of the life that is truly life."

Tithing in the Old Testament established rules for proportionate giving but today, anybody dedicated to the church should be able to offer an appropriate portion of money voluntarily to support the ongoing operation of the ministry, therefore the Old Covenant of keeping the law to gain forgiveness is fulfilled in the New Covenant, which is the New Law in the Gospel of Grace. Apostle Paul, makes it clear that generosity should be cheerful and voluntary, according to 2 Corinthians 9:6-7 that says, "Remember this: Whoever sows sparingly will also reap sparingly, and whoever sows generously will also reap generously. Each man should give what he has decided in his heart, to give, not reluctantly or under compulsion, for God loves a cheerful giver. And God is able to make all grace abound to you, so that in all things at all times, having all that you need; you will abound in every good work. As it is written: He has scattered abroad his gifts to the poor his righteousness endures forever." So, we should not allow the Old Covenant law of tithing become a stumbling block to embrace the New Covenant behavior of generosity, because if some people want to give only one cent and work their way up to give more, so be it, it's a tax write off anyway. The pressure of giving is why some people do not attend church because they feel guilty of not having any money to give, the subject of God's law and commandment has been twisted and mangled by some pastors beyond recognition because the love for God is not money. According to 1 John 5:3-12 that says, "This is love for God: To obey his commands. And his commands are not burdensome, for everyone born of God overcomes the world.

49

This is the victory that has overcome the world, even our faith. Who is it that overcomes the world? Only he who believes that Jesus is the Son of God. This is the one who came by water and blood – Jesus Christ. He did not come by water only, but by water and blood. And it is the Spirit who testifies, because the Spirit is the truth. For there are three that testify: The Spirit, the Water, and the Blood; and the three are in agreement. We accept man's testimony, but God's testimony is greater because it is the testimony of God, which He has given His Son. Anyone who believes in the Son of God, has this testimony in his heart. Anyone who does not believe God has made him out to be a liar, because he has not believed the testimony that God given about His Son. And this is the testimony: God has given us eternal life, and this life is in his Son. He who has the Son has life; he who does not have the Son of God, does not have life."

The Hebrew Bible Called:
ETH CEPHER

In this book we will find the Set-Apart Scriptures, a comprehensive restoration of scripture including: All of the previously canonized text, all of the Deuterocanon/Apocryphal text, the Books of Jubilees, Enoch, Jasher, 3 Ezra and 4 Ezra (1 Esdras and 2 Esdras) – for the total of 87 books versus 66 books, actually, the historic facts of the Hebrew Nation. And this book is translated in the English version however, you will come across the name of God's in Hebrew – Yahuah (for the Father), Yahusah (for his Son), and Ruach Ha'Qodesh (for the Holy Spirit) also, we learn that these names is known by all of the prophets of the Old and New Testament. And will discover that it was "He" who visited Moses at the burning bush "I AM WHO I AM" and according to the ETH CEPHER – (known as the Divine Book and the Hebrew Bible) in Exodus 34, Moses returned to the top of Mt. Sinai – there the Lord appeared to him, revealing not only his glory but also his name – Yahuah. Which appears in the English translation as "LORD" which is related to the etymologically - meaning; true sense or sense of the truth. The study of the origin of word "Yahuah" and its meaning changed over the history of the world.

Yah – is the shortened name for Yahuah – which means "He" and Ushua or Usha – means to make equal therefore Yahusha or Yahushua – means "He" who made equal, and if we connected "uah" to the back of Yah – it means the "Breath" of God or Spirit, within His own name – Ruach Elohiym (Spirit of God), which is the: Ruach Ha'Qodesh or the Holy Spirit. Hebrew is the original inspired language of the Old Testament, therefore the word "Ruach" can be construed as a person, also known as the "Invisible Wind" or the "Everlasting Fire" which was presented in front of Moses and he felt the power. It's the "Breath of God" which is His disperses: His life-force, His energy and intention that's omnipresent. And can be directed in a specific way for a specific purpose that remains outside of our physical dimension, but in the Hebrew language the word "Ruach" is feminine! And in contrast to the name "Lord" is found at least 175 times in the "Tanakh or Torah" which is the Old Testament of the King James Version of the Bible. But the name "YAHUAH" is found well over 175 times in the Eth CEPHER or the Hebrew Bible. The Story of Susanna can easily relates to our generation because this story explains why we cannot believe everything that we hear without proof, our Heavenly Father, informed his children to test everything to see if it's true. According to the Eth CEPHER in 1 Thessalonians 5:21 that says, "Prove all things; hold fast that which is good."

53

Biblical scholar translators are hoping to have the Bible in every language around the world soon, but as long man and woman are translating the Bible, they're going to be some errors however, there's no Bible, better than the anyother but it's especially important to get as close as possible to the truth. So, I encourage the reader of this book to watch the documentary that's called: Whited Out III on YouTube. The Eth CEPHER restores the original names and places that the King James Bible, don't do! And if we really want to find the name of God, the only thing we have to do is open this book to Exodus 3:13-15 that says, "And Mosheh (Moses) said unto Elohiym, behold, when I come unto the children of Yashar'el (Israel) and shall say unto them, the Elohai (God) of your fathers has sent me unto you; and they shall say to me: What is his name? What shall I say unto them? And Elohiym said unto El-Mosheh (Moses), Ehayah Asher Ehayah (I Am Who I Am); and he said, thus shall you say unto the children of Yashar'el (Israel) Ehayah (I Am) has sent me unto you. And Elohiym said moreover unto El-Moshen (Moses) thus shall you say unto the children of Yashar'el (Israel). Yahuah Elohai (God) of you fathers, the Elohai (God) of Avraham (Abraham), the Elohai (God) of Yitschaq (Isaac), and the Elohai (God) of Ya'aqov (Jacob), has sent me unto you; this is my name forever, and this is my mention (citing or calling attention to) unto all generations." The question is this: In the King James Bible, did Jesus, used the word "I Am" to represented himself as God, anytime in his ministry while he was on earth?

In the New Testament, according to the NIV Quiet Time Bible in John 8:58 says, "I tell you the truth, Jesus answered, before Abraham was born, I am!" So, in the NIV Quiet Time Bible even in the King James Bible: Jesus; clearly identifies himself as – God! According to the Eth CEPHER in Deuteronomy 32:1-6 that says, "Give ear, O ye heavens, and I will speak; and hear, O earth, the words of my mouth. My doctrine shall drop as the rain, my speech shall distil as the dew, as the small rain upon the tender herb, and as the showers upon the grass: Because I will publish the name of YAHUAH: ascribe ye greatness unto our Elohiym. He is the Rock, his work is perfect; for all his ways are judgment; an El of Truth and without iniquity, just and right is he. They have corrupted themselves; their spot is not the spot of his children; they are a perverse and crooked generation. Do ye thus requite YAHUAH, O foolish people and unwise? Is not he your Father, that has bought you? Has he not made you, and established you?" When we pray, we have God attention especially because of His Holy Spirit, that live in us – the Spirit of God, this is why He recognize His children as His "Bride" that incredible gift – is the Holy Spirit. The trajectory of our life is nothing without prayer and it's the least utilized gift that God ever gave his children to establish a sustainable connection with Him and His Son. The Messiah or His Son; made it easier for us to talk to our Heavenly Father. And our mind is not capable of understanding the amount of power we possess when we pray, this is why the devil finds ways to distract our prayer life, and keep us not only in the dark but sometime powerless against his attacks.

55

The solving of every problem starts with having a prayer life, this is where we can meet every needs, the answer to fight every battle, the strength to accomplish our golds and find our purpose, yes, all of this is wrapped up in having a Godly prayer life with our Heavenly Father. Meyshak, Shadrak and Aved Nego prayed - The Prayer of Azaiah: They pray for help and deliverance. This is the type of prayer life that we need today for help and deliverance and to overcome our enemies, according to the Eth CEPHER, the prayer that was spoken in the Fiery Furnace – oh, remember they were Hebrews; praying to their God. Blessed are you, O Yahuah Elohiym of our fathers; your name is worthy to be praised and glorified forevermore; for you are righteous in all the things that you have done to us. Yes, true are all your works, your ways are right, and all your judgments truth. In all the things that you have brought upon us, and upon the Holy City of our fathers even Yerushalayim (Jerusalem), you have executed true judgment; for according to the truth and judgment did you bring all these things upon us because of our sins. For we have sinned and committed iniquity, departing from you. In all things have we trespassed, and not obeyed your commandments, nor kept them, neither done as you have commanded us, that it might go well with us. Wherefore all that you have brought upon us, you have done in true judgment. And you did deliver us into the hands of Torahless enemies most hateful forsakers of Elohyim, and to an unjust king, and the most wicked in all the world. And now we cannot open our mouths, we are become a shame and reproach to your servants; and to them that worship you.

Yet deliver us not up wholly, for your name's sake, neither disannul your covenant: And cause not your mercy to depart from us, for your beloved Avraham's (Abraham's) sake, for your servant Yitschq's (Isaac) sake, and for your Holy Yashar'el (Israel) sake; to whom you spoken and promised that you would multiply their descendants (seed) as the stars of heaven, and as the sand that lies upon the seashore. For we, O YAHUAH, are become less than any nation, and be kept under this day in all the world because of our sins. Neither is there at this time prince, or prophet, or leader, or ascending smoke offering, or sacrifice, or oblation, or incense or place to sacrifice before you, and to find mercy. Nevertheless, in a contrite heart and a humble ruach let us be accepted. Like as in the ascending smoke offerings of rams and bullocks and like in ten thousand of fat lambs: So, let our sacrifice be in your sight this day, and grant that we may wholly go after you: For they shall not be confounded that put their trust in you. And now we follow you with all our heart, we fear you, and seek your face. Put us not to shame: But deal with us after your lovingkindness, and according to the multitude of your mercies. Deliver us also according to your marvelous works, and give glory to your name, O YAHUAH: and let all them that do your servants hurt be ashamed; and let them be confounded in all their power and might, and let their strength be broken; and let them know that you are Elohiym, the only Elohiym, and glorious over the whole world."

And according to the Eth CEPHER, God – personal name is: Elohayka or Yahuah and His son's name is: Yahusha – His actually name means; to be open (awaken), wide or free, to avenge, to defend, to deliver, to help, to preserve, to rescue, to bring or to have salvation, to save or to be a savior and get victory. This name is the most accurate name that was translated from one scripture to another, mapping from one system of writing to another, swapping letters in a predicable way such as in the Greek and Latin language. We were informed that biblical literature has three bodies of written: The Old Testament writing according to the Hebrew people and the practice Judaism as a religion – the Torah. The Apocrypha, which some people consider intertestamental work, and the New Testament – the Birth of the Church and the early dissemination of Christianity. Without the Old Testament there's no New Testament, and this love letter from God and the redemption for mankind would not be. These books contain historically factual information or adequate accounts of the universe and the beginning of all Creation. Knowledgement of Wisdom: That furnish a profoundly theological interpretation of God as God, and His existence as the One and Only Almighty God. The Church have a responsibility driven by the power of biblical themes to teach social responsibility to the children of God, by obeying his New Laws – the Commandments, to have love for all mankind, to have citizenship in the family of God, to have rights in the Kingdom yet to come and this is viewed as the gracious and mercy works of God or other words paying tithes and our offering is offering a helping hand.

Furthermore, each biblical book within it has its own history, and the translation techniques is stylistic characteristics that must be examined and considered to be read with great caution because of the proper methodology: A particular procedure or set of procedures. Remember, the meta-narrative story of the Bible; is about salvation through the Son of God – and the comprehensive view of "Love" that God, has for His creation. Knowing this; all the story of the Bible is nothing but one big story of restoration and the Kingdom of God, that's coming. So, the meta-narrative of the Bible, is the absolute universal truth! According to the NIV Quiet Time Bible in Ephesians 2:14-20 that says, "For He himself is our peace, who has made the two, one and has destroyed the barrier, the dividing wall of hostility, by abolishing in his flesh the law with its commandment and regulations. His purpose was to create in himself one new man, out of the two, thus making peace, and in this one body to reconcile both of them to God through the cross, by which he put to death their hostility. He came and preached peace to you who were far away and peace to those who were near. For through him we both have access to the Father by one Spirit. Consequently, you are no longer foreigners and aliens, but fellow citizens with God's people and members of God's household, built on the foundation of the apostles and prophets, with Christ Jesus himself as the chief cornerstone." And biblical speaking the King James Bible got approved in 1604 by forty-seven scholars at Westminster, Oxford and Cambridge but was not published until 1611.

However, the latest version of the Bible was to be preserve as vulgarly (in a way that does not have used forms of proper names, in keeping with its aim to make or show good taste, for example: They vulgarly display their wealth by purchasing flashy and expensive cars). The scriptures popular and familiar superior to the Greek original but contained errors. Therefore by the 18th century the King James Version had supplanted the Great Bible and the Geneva Bible – which is the English translation published the New Testament in 1557 and the Old Testament in 1560, by a colony of Protestant scholars in exile from England who worked under the general direction of Miles Coverdale and John Knox and under the influence of John Calvin. The English churchmen had fled London during the repressive reign of the Roman Catholic – Mary I (Queen of England), which had halted the publication of the Bible there: The Geneva Bible before the 20th century was regarded as a masterpiece of English-language literature. But by the late 20th century it had become the favorite translation of English-speaking Christian, some of whom regarded it as divinely inspired but still had some typographical errors. Another innovation was formatted in the United States, from the works of the British scholars was submitted and the instruction to the committees made clear that only a revision, not a new translation was contemplated, so, the New Testament was published in Britain on May 17, 1881 and three days later in the United States, after 11 years of labor.

Over 30,000 changes were made, of which more than 5,000 represent differences between the Greek text used for the Revised Version, and that used as the basis of the King James Version, and most of the other changes were made in the interest of consistency or modernization. And the Old Testament went publication in 1885, stirred far less excitement because it was less well known than the New Testament. Which needed fewer changes especially the Book of Job, the Poetic, the Prophetic, Ecclesiastes and Isaiah because these books benefited greatly. And the revision of the Apocrypha, not originally contemplated, came to be included only because of copyright arrangements made with the university presses of Oxford and Cambridge and was first published in 1865. In 1928, the copyright of the American Standard Version was acquired by the International Council of Religious Education and thereby passed into the ownership of churches representing forty major denominations in the United States and Canada. A two year study by special committee recommended a revision, and in 1937 the council gave its authorization to the proposal but not until 1946, did the revision of the New Testament appear in print and six years later the complete revised of the Bible (RSV) was published and not until 1952, a decision was made to translate the Apocrypha and a revision appeared in 1957. However, under a joint committee representing the major Protestant churches of the British Isles, with the Roman Catholics appointed as observers, the New Testament was published in 1961, and a second edition of the Old and the New Testament along with the Apocrypha was published in 1970.

The International Bible Society undertook the translation and produced the New Testament in 1973 and then completed the entire Bible in 1978, scholars from various Protestant traditions participated. And the New International Version (NIV) subsequently became the best-selling English language translation by the early 21st century and the most popular with Evangelicals. Even though some scholars raised concerns about the rendering of some key passages of Scripture, most notably in Apostle Paul's letters which they felt had been distorted by an overt evangelical agenda, furthermore, an attempt at introducing gender-sensitive language attracted such antipathy that a 1997 revision was abandoned. A gender-inclusive in Today's New International Version (TNIV) attracted the scorn of traditionalists however in 2011 the NIV was revised again, this time to much broader acceptance by traditionalists therefore some fundamentalist denominations such as the Southern Baptist Convention, rejected the new translation. And we have the New King James Version (NKJV) which was published and completed in 1983, that gained popularity among Bible societies than the New Revised Standard Version (NRSV) around 1995. Biblically the meta-narrative of the Bible, is the comprehensive idea behind the story that's common to all people, about all the creation of the world. That explains events that took place in the heavens and on earth, with some angels falling from grace and some angels decided to be disobedience to God by taking human wives, however the Great Flood initiated the redemption with mankind.

We are called to assemble or to assembly, who are crafted into the family of God, by the blood of the Passover Lamb, which is the Messiah. For the purpose of walking in faith not into the narrative of the world, but to do all that we can, which is right or righteous according to the Grace of God: Which have a lot to do with His Salvation, Sanctification and Glorification that we should celebrates the Messiah ministry and the gospel of His - New Law. However today the word "Church" is used to describe a building but in the New Testament, this word means "Ecclesia" (which means the called-out ones) as one community of people all over the world living in one kingdom with the Spirit of God, reigns in our hearts. Now, the meta-narrative of the word church; is our body. According to the NIV Quiet Time Bible says in 1 Corinthians 1:10-19 "I appeal to you, brothers, in the name of our Lord Jesus Christ, that all of you agree with one another so that there may be no divisions among you and that you may be perfectly united in mind and thought. My brothers, some from Chloe's household, have informed me that there are quarrels among you. What I mean is this: One of you says, I follow Paul, another, I follow Apollos, another, I follow Cephas, still another, I follow Christ. Is Christ divided? Was Paul crucified for you? Were you baptized into the name of Paul? I am thankful that I did not baptize any of you except Crispus and Gaius, so no one can say that you were baptized in my name. (Yes, I also baptized the household of Stephanas; beyond that, I don't remember if I baptized anyone else).

For Christ did not send me to baptize, but to preach the gospel – not with words of human wisdom, lest the cross of Christ be emptied of its power. For the message of the cross is foolishness to those who are perishing, but to us who are being saved it is the power of God. For it is written: I will destroy the wisdom of the wise; the intelligence of the intelligent I will frustrate." Know this: Our Messiah loves His church because He died for His church, so we have to distinguish between an organizational structure and the reality of the Spirit of God, because the word church has evolved due to the work of men. However, today churches are a 501©3 organization or a charity although it's worth pointing out that many people use the term non-profit, but a non-profit is an entity that is organized for a non-commercial purpose, no matter the legal structure the key element is its non-commercial nature. Some churches may be commercial in nature if they have a bookstore, offering exercise classes or promoting a healthy lifestyle in the name of religion. So, are today churches a 501©3, well, the answer can be a little complicated! Because 501©3 section of the U.S. tax code describes non-profits that are charitable in nature meaning every time you give in a way that is monetary gift either at the end of the year or during church service; the people should get a receipt of the amount of money that they donated and this will allow the people to claim the monetary gift on their income tax returns.

Churches are religious organizations that qualify to be non-profit regardless of the corporate structure, therefore the church is able to provide its donors with a potential tax-deduction for their gifts giving. Now, this is the complicated part: The government is over the churches, yes, over the churches? Because 501©3 was created as a tool to put the church under their control, particularly the IRS – when applying for and receiving their determination letter. The churches have essentially ceded control of their church, to the IRS, instead of God! The churches organize as a 508©1(a) free of tax-exempt not having any accountability but to the IRS, however if the churches don't choose to be a 501(c) 3, then if simply will be treated like a taxable profit business. According to the NIV Quiet Time Bible in Matthew 19:16-19 that says, "Now a man came up to Jesus and asked: Teacher, what good thing must I do to get eternal life? Why do you ask me about what is good? Jesus replied. There is only One who is good. If you want (eternal life), obey the commandments. (This is our tithes)! Which ones? The man inquired. Jesus replied: Do not murder, Do not commit adultery, Do not steal, Do not give false testimony, Honor your Father and Mother, and Love your neighbor as yourself." (Replace; the word "Love" with "Respect" and we will get the same meaning). And in Matthew 22:34-40 that says, "Hearing that Jesus had silenced the Sadducees, the Pharisees got together. One of them, an expert in the law, tested him with this question: Teacher, which is the greatest commandment in the law? Jesus replied: Love the Lord your God with all your heart and with all your soul and with all your mind.

This is the first and greatest commandment. And the second is like it: Love your neighbor as yourself. All the Law and the Prophet hang on these two commandments." Understand this: Our ancestors survived slavery in order for the Black race to gain citizenship and the right to vote. They went through treacherous conditions, just for us to have opportunities in this great country called: America. English was not their first language but with each generation we speak this language better and better, with addition education we have an opportunity to learn other languages. Now, is the time to wake up! And recognize that the truth is in the Scriptures, according to the NIV Quiet Time Bible in Revelation 3:1-3 that says, "To the angel of the church in Sardis write: These are the words of him who holds the Seven Spirits of God and the Seven Stars. I know your deeds; you have a reputation of being alive, but you are dead. Wake up! Strengthen what remains and is about to die, for I have not found your deeds complete in the sight of my God. Remember, therefore, what you have received and heard; obey it, and repent. But if you do not wake up, I will come like a thief, and you will not know at what time I will come to you." Please: If you have never read the Book of Daniel, Ch. 12 please, do so! It's one of those chapters that will remind us of what's to come, and it will help us to focus on our daily bread on living in the moment. According to the NIV Quiet Time Bible in Daniel 12:1-4 that says, "At that time Michael; the Great Prince, who protects your people will arise.

There will be a time of distress such as has not happened from the beginning on nations until then. But at that time your people – everyone whose name is found written in the book – will be delivered: Multitudes who sleep in the dust of the earth will awake; some to everlasting life, others to shame and everlasting contempt. Those who are wise will shine like the brightness of the heavens, and those who lead many to righteousness, like the stars forever and ever. But you, Daniel, close up and seal the words of the scroll until the time of the end. Many will go here and there to increase knowledge." Although our main request, should be that our names are found in the book of life, we should pray that we don't escape from the distress that's to come, because how can our faith be tested. And this is another reason the morning and the evening sacrifice are important, which is the Lord Prayer. And according to Act 2:17-21 that says, "In the last days, God says, I will pour out my Spirit on all people: Your sons and daughters will prophesy, your young men will see visions, your old men will dream dreams. Even on my servants, both men and women, I will pour out my Spirit in those days, and they will prophesy. I will show wonders in heaven above and signs on the earth below, blood and fire and billows of smoke. The sun will be turned to darkness and the moon to blood before the coming of the great and glorious day of the Lord. And everyone who calls on the name of the Lord will be saved."

We have seen these signs in the sky and what a shame if believer do not recognize the signs and the outpouring of the Spirit and the wonderful blessing that God has for his children, sorry to say that time is now and we're running out of time because our Messiah is going sneak up on us like a thief in the night, if we're not watching also paying attention to God wonderful signs. We cannot let distractions be our downfall and please; we must get an understanding about perception because it's not reality! We will find ourselves guilty of bearing false witness and creating strongholds by tearing a person down in doing the work of the devil. And it is the devil, that's encouraging God's children to create a false reality by using God words again us, by telling us that we have the power to create with our words, so, he is encouraging God children to lie, it is he, that's telling us to create your own reality. Perception is just a mirage it's a figment of your imagination keeping God's children trap in sin by spreading lies and it's in violation of the second greatest commandment because love is another word for respect; so how can we love our neighbor if we don't respect them, so remember when we respect our neighbor we are showing love. Know this: It does not matter how many people say the same old lie, it's still a lie! Hating is the image and likeness of the devil and he loves that kind of energy, because it is the opposite of love. Our emotions can carry spiritual strongholds that can kill, steal, and destroy a person life, character and reputation.

According to the NIV Quiet Time Bible in 2 Corinthians 10:3-6 that says, "For though we live in the world, we do not wage war as the world does: The weapons we fight with are not the weapons of the world. On the contrary, they have divine power to demolish strongholds. We demolish arguments and every pretension that sets itself up against the knowledge of God, and we take captive every thought to make it obedient to Christ. And we will be ready to punish every act of disobedience, once your obedience is complete." And what weapon do we need to demolish the mental or emotional stronghold of the devil? It's the Bible, the living Word of God, will shatter strongholds of every kind that will keep a person hostage from escaping spiritual battle of the devil. In the spiritual world perception is a strong demon, a wicked tyrant that tries to rule over their subjects by bullying them with lies, and he will try to steal everything that's good and have no problem bring in reinforcements to support his lie. And in Ephesians 6:10-18 that says, "Finally, be strong in the Lord and in his mighty power. Put on the full armor of God so that you can take your stand against the devil's schemes. For our struggle is not against flesh and blood, but against the rulers, against the authorities, against the powers of this dark world and against the spiritual forces of evil in the heavenly realms. Therefore, put on the full armor of God, so that when the day of evil comes, you may be able to stand your ground, and after you have done everything, to stand. Stand firm then, with the belt of truth buckled around your waist, with the breastplate of righteousness in place, and with your feet fitted with the readiness that comes from the gospel of peace.

In addition to all this, take up the shield of faith, with which you can extinguish all the flaming arrows of the evil one. Take the helmet of salvation and the sword of the Spirit, which is the word of God. And pray in the Spirit on all occasions with all kinds of prayers and requests. With this in mind, be alert and always keep on praying for all the saints." Here's a prayer that will help bring down strongholds: Thank you Heavenly Father, for giving the world your Son, and He made a promise to us that He will not forsake us in the time of trouble; it's your Son, that's uplifting and encouraging us day and night. Heavenly Father, I agree with the Gospel of Grace and Salvation that your - Son, brought into this world because He reflects you! Which is love, and I know that He love me and I will show my love back to you Heavenly Father by keeping your commandments. Heavenly Father, it's you that sees beyond the veil, and it's you that tear down every stronghold of the devil scheme that tries to kill, steal, and destroy every believer life. I yearn for you to gaze into my life and over my family's life; it's you that encouraging your children to put on your armor for protection from the devil. When you look down on us from your heavenly throne, it's you that see all of our troubles including our inner-most hurts, struggles, pain and fears. I'm grateful for the relationship that I have with you Heavenly Father, in the name and the authority of the Son and your Spirit, that dwell over our life.

We will speak the priestly blessing that's in the Book of Numbers 6:22-27 that says, "The LORD said to Moses: Tell Aaron and his sons, this is how you are to bless the Israelites, say to them: The LORD bless you and keep you; the LORD make his face shine upon you and be gracious to you; the LORD turn his face toward you and give you peace. So, they will put my name on the Israelites, and I will bless them." Heavenly Father, please make this my reality that your face will shine on me day and night and give me peace because your eyes are filled with compassion and mercy and with unconditional love and it's your embrace that makes me stand up straight. Heavenly Father, I close out this prayer by saying: I acknowledge that I need your help to have victory over this mental battle called: Life. And you didn't created your children to be bound and crippled by fear, loneliness, rejection, un-forgiveness, lust, bitterness, anxiety, doubt, low self-esteem, guilt, insecurities, having bad addiction, suicidal thoughts, anger, self-defeating and judgmental thoughts because your desire is for your children to live a life of free will. According to the New Law! So, Heavenly Father, teach your children; how to control and conquer my thoughts and tear down every strongholds that is trying to take control over our mind: Heavenly Father I come to you, in the authority of your Son and the Spirit of You – the Holy Spirit, Amein   (It   is   so).

America Strong
The Book of Mormon

The Book of Mormon is the Word of God! And clearly, this book has a lot to say about the prophets, revelation, and the principal business of the Messiah. The prophet of old has mistakenly been thought to foretell coming events which some people may call prophecies. However a prophet does a lot more than tell the future, one of the key phrases of the prophet is "Thus said the LORD or It is Written" these phrase appear over forty times in the Book of Mormon and commonly used in the Bible. They use this phrase because the prophets are the messengers from God, and they are revealing what they received, and this is called: Revelation! Reading the Book of Mormon will add key principles in your life that will cause you to treat other with love, respect and become a better version of yourself but the best part of reading the Book of Mormon. Is, it was written right here in America, about people of color known as the Lost Sheep of God: Using his prophets to reveal the coming of the Messiah, about his birth, his ministry, his death and his resurrection but the most powerful meta-narrative about this story is when He revealed himself to the people, the lost sheep. Christ refers to these as the lost sheep of the house of Israel.

The Bible and the Book of Mormon are the two witnesses, that support each other about God's planned for redemption and his coming kingdom and when I talk about the Book of Mormon, please, don't be confused because I'm not talking about the religious - Mormons! It's all about the book because it brings forth marvelous works on the things that hidden and the authorship of the Messiah, which is Salvation! This book is the most self-conscious book that anyone will ever read because its purpose is to bring the reader closer to God, while He reveal His Son to the world. According to the NIV Quiet Time Bible in John 10:16-18 that says, "I have other sheep that are not of this sheep pen. I must bring them also: They too will listen to my voice, and there shall be one flock and one shepherd. The reason my Father loves me is that I lay down my life – only to take it up again. No one takes it from me, but I lay it down of my own accord. I have the authority to lay it down and authority to take it up again. This command I received from my Father." According to the Book of Mormon in 1 Nephi 6:4 that says, "For the fullness of mine intent is that I may persuade men to come unto the God of Abraham, and the God of Isaac and the God of Jacob and be saved." God instructed His prophets in this land called: America, to keep records of His teaching and the law in writing. They were eventually gathered into one book by a prophet named Mormon, and this book affirms the life of the Son of God – and his ministry, the act of salvation, and his overcoming his death; are the highlights in the Book of Mormon. Scholars, said the 1840 Edition Book of Mormon was written by Joseph Smith – a Gentile, meaning he was a non-Jewish person.

Who authored the Book of Mormon in English by divine wisdom – the Ruach Ha'Qoseh – the Holy Spirit. Joseph Smith, discovered the golden plates that was written by the hand of the Prophet Mormon and his son Moroni, according to the title page of the Book of Mormon: Wherefore, it is an abridgment of the record of the people of Nephi, and also of the Lamanites – written to the Lamanites, who are a remnant of the House of Israel: Also to the Gentile. To come forth by the gift and power of God, unto the interpretation thereof sealed by the hand of Moroni, and hid up by God, to come forth in due time by the way of the Gentile. The Book of Mormon is about the people who lived beyond the geographical setting outside the Mediterranean area and what kind of interaction they had with God, even Apostle Paul taught according to 2 Corinthians 13:1 that says, "This will be my third visit to you: Every matter must be established by the testimony of two or three witnesses." When God teaches an important principle, He sends another source to confirm it. The Book of Mormon is the second witness to the Bible teachings, but keeping it real; both the Bible and the Book of Mormon testify to the Messiah, as the Son of God, who brought the Gospel of Grace to the children of God. And both describe God's interactions with his children in two different area of the world but teaching the same principles. However the Book of Mormon confirm what the Bible says; about the Messiah but please get an understanding of the region of the world that he was born in! The story is true, but the name and skin color has been change.

According to the Book of Mormon in Mormon 7:8-9 that says, "For behold, this is written for the intent that ye may believe and if ye believe that ye will believe this also; and if ye believe this ye will know concerning your fathers, and also the marvelous works which were wrought by the power of God among them." The Prophet Mormon engraved the abridgement on gold plates in a language of his people that were called: Reformed Egyptians. This is why the book carries his name – Mormon, but at the end of his life, he passed these engraved plates to his son – Moroni. Who was also a prophet of God, and was the last to add to his father, book. However, it was said that right before Moroni died, he buried the gold plates in a box on a hillside near what is now call upstate New York. But in 1823 it was said; that the spirit of Moroni, appeared to Joseph Smith and spoke to him about the plates also showed Joseph Smith where to find them, and he was to translate the record into English: Which he did under the power and inspiration of the Holy Spirit. So, let's identify who is Nephi – he was a prophet, the son of Lehi and his mother was Sariah. He also had three brothers Leman, Lemuel and Sam and their story started off in Jerusalem, similar to the story of Abraham. God called on Lehi to depart out of the land of Jerusalem, because of the people iniquity. Lehi, was a prophet just like Abraham, he took his family and all the people that was willing to leave with him out of the land. During the course of their travels, they came to a large body of water and God commanded Lehi, to build a ship to cross over into the Promised Land.

According to the Book of Mormon in Nephi 1:1 that says, "I, Nephi, having been born of godly parents, therefore, I was taught somewhat in all the learning of my father, and having seen many afflictions in the course of my days, nevertheless having been highly favored of the Almighty Creator, in all my days; yea, having had a great knowledge of the goodness and the mysteries of God, therefore, I make a record of my proceeding in my days." And in Nephi 1:4 that says, "For it came to pass in the commencement of the first year of the reign of Zedekiah – the King of Judah, my father Lehi, having dwelt at Jerusalem in all his days and in the same year there came many prophet, prophesying unto the people that they must repent or the great city Jerusalem must be destroyed." As we read on: Nephi 1:6-17 and verse 19 says, "And it came to pass as he (Lehi) prayed unto God, there came a pillar of fire and dwelt upon a rock before him; and he saw and heard much and because of the things which he saw and heard he did quake and tremble exceedingly. And it came to pass that he returned to his own house at Jerusalem, and he cast himself upon his bed, being overcome with the Spirit of God, and the things which he had seen. He was carried away in a vision, even that he saw the heavens open, and he saw God sitting upon his throne surrounded with numberless concourses of angels in the attitude of singing and praising their God. And it came to pass that he saw One descending out of the midst of heaven, and he beheld that his luster was above that of the sun at noon day. And he also saw twelve others following him and their brightness did exceed that of the stars in the firmament.

And they came down and went forth upon the face of the earth; and the first came and stood before my father and gave unto him a book and bade him, that he should read, saying: Wo Wo, unto Jerusalem, for I have seen thine abominations! Yes, and many things did my father read concerning Jerusalem, that it should be destroyed, and the inhabitants thereof; many should perish by the sword, and many should be carried away captive into Babylon. And it came to pass that when my father had read and seen many great and marvelous things, he did exclaim many things unto God, such as: Great and Marvelous are the works, O God Almighty! Thy throne is high in the heavens and thy power and goodness, and mercy are over all the inhabitants of the earth and because thou are merciful, thou wilt not suffer those who come unto thee that they shall perish!" And after this manner was the language of my father (Hebrew) in the praising of his God; for his soul did rejoice, and his whole heart was filled because of the things which he had seen, yes, which God had shown unto him. And now, I Nephi, do not make a full account of the things which my father hath written, for he hath written many things which he saw in visions and in dreams; and he also hath written many things which he prophesied and speak unto his children, of which I shall not make a full account. But I shall make an account of my proceedings in my days. Behold, I make an abridgment of the record on my father, upon plates which I have made with mine own hands, wherefore, after I have abridged the record of my father then will I make an account of my own life."

According to the Book of Mormon in Nephi 1:19 that says, "And it came to pass that the Jews, did mock Lehi, because of the things which he testified of them; for he truly testified of their wickedness and their abominations and he testified that the things which he saw and heard and also the things which he read in the book, manifested plainly of the coming Messiah and the redemption of the world." According to the Book of Mormon in 2 Nephi 3:6 that says, "For Joseph (son of Lehi) truly testified, saying: A seer shall the Lord my God raise up, who shall be a choice seer unto the fruit of my loins." One of Joseph Smith's functions was to re-establish the concept of God and His Covenant: But what is amazing that - Joseph Smith role was to establish a covenant of consciousness among the Gentiles. And in 2 Nephi 3:8 that says, "And I will give unto him a commandment that he shall do none other work, save the work which I shall command him. And I will make him great in my eyes; for he shall do my work." The Book of Mormon and the Bible, especially the Old Testament is joined together to make one stick these two great records speak of the promises that was made about the gathering of the House of Israel and of the House of Judah: And in the Book of Ezekiel, chapter 38, talks about Gog of Magog and the destruction which will precede the Second Coming. One of the major functions of the Book of Mormon is to prove to the world that the Holy Scriptures of the Bible are true! According to the Book of Mormon in Mosiah 13:33-35 that says, "For behold, did not Moses prophesy unto them concerning the coming of the Messiah, and that God should redeem his people?

Yes, and even all the prophets who have prophesied ever since the world began – have they not spoken more or less concerning these things? Have they not said that God himself should come down among the children of men, and take upon him the form of man, and go forth in mighty power upon the face of the earth? Yes, and have they not said also that he should bring to pass the resurrection of the dead, and that he, himself, should be oppressed and afflicted?" And in Mosiah 16:15 that says, "Teach them that redemption cometh through Christ the Lord, who is the Eternal Father, Amen." Can anyone imagine that God had prophets all over the world, as if He was playing chess with the devil? According to the Book of Mormon in Alma 34:5 that says, "And we have beheld that the great question which is in your minds is whether the word be in the Son of God, or whether there shall be no Christ." And in verses 9-10 that says, "For it is expedient that an atonement should be made; for according to the great plan of the Eternal God there must be an atonement made, or else all mankind must unavoidably perish except it be through the atonement which it is expedient should be made. For it is expedient that there should be a great and last sacrifice; yes, not a sacrifice of man, neither of beast, neither of any manner of fowl; for it shall not be a human sacrifice; but it must be an infinite and eternal sacrifice."

He is not to be bound by time but metaphysics – the branch of philosophy that deals with the first principles of things, including abstract concepts such as being, knowing, substance, cause, identity, time, and space. One thing about metaphysicians its claim the natural of science and investigates the universe of experience, while concern aspects of reality that transcend the truth. But the danger is that any attempt to go beyond the experience ends up meaningless, and as human we cannot make no sense of God eternal infinite. Therefore, what makes these two book testify to each other is the scripture starting with the Book of Mormon in 2 Nephi 25:23 that says "For we labor diligently to write, to persuade our children, and also our brethren to believe in Christ, and to be reconciled to God; for we know that it is by grace that we are saved, after all we can do." Now the key phrase is "after all we can do" meaning that we must do all that we can do that is right, and this is our obligation to God of paying tithes called: Righteousness! And in the NIV Quiet Time Bible in Ephesians 2:1-10 that says "As for you, you were dead in your transgressions and sins, in which you used to live when you followed the ways of this world and of the ruler of the kingdom of the air, the spirit who is now at work in those who are disobedient. All of us also lived among them at one time, gratifying the cravings of our sinful nature and following its desires and thoughts. Like the rest, we were by nature objects of wrath. But because of his great love for us, God, who is rich in mercy, made us alive with Christ even when we were dead in transgressions – it is by grace you have been saved.

And God raised us up with Christ and seated us with him in the heavenly realms in Christ Jesus, in order thatin the coming ages he might show the incomparable riches of his grace, expressed in his kindness to us in Christ Jesus. For it is by grace you have been saved, through faith – and this not from yourselves, it is the gift of God – not by works, so that no one can boast. For we are God's workmanship, created in Christ Jesus to do good works, which God prepared in advance for us to do." Also in the Eth CEPHER in Ephesians 2:7-10 that says, "That in the ages to come he might show the exceeding riches of his grace in his kindness toward us through Mashiach Yahusha (Salvation in the Messiah). For by grace are ye saved through faith; and that not of yourselves – it is the gift of Elohiym: Not of works, lest any man should boast – for we are his workmanship, created in Mashiach Yahusha unto good works, which Elohiym has before ordained that we should walk in them." Therefore, what these three different scriptures are saying: That we are completely saved by the Gospel of Grace, through Faith, not of works, but a gift from God through his Son. This is why these two books are important to read outside the King James Bible. In the Book of Mormon in 3 Nephi Chapter 9, 10 and 11 – testify sometime after the death of the Messiah: Christ appeared to the people of Nephites in the ancient land called – America. As multitude of people gather together in the land of Bountiful.

He did minister unto them and baptized them and proclaiming His atonement, they felt His wounds and in His hands, feet and on His side, but the first thing that He say, according to the Book of Mormon in 3 Nephi 11:10 was, "Behold, I am (the Messiah – the Son of God) whom the prophets testified shall come into the world." The important of the anticipation of the Book of Mormon culminates the appearances and the resurrected of the Messiah marvelously, reported in 3 Nephi 11:10. The Prophet Mormon masterfully crafted the Book of Mormon to point out the supreme moment when Christ would come and heal His lost sheep but throughout the narrative, he informed many who closed themselves off from God; that someday Christ would come to heal humanity. The Prophet Mormon carefully and deliberately alluded to the words of Isaiah to forcefully illustrate that the pinnacle of the Old Testament, that the majestic moment had arrived with the words "I Am." According to the Book of Mormon in 3 Nephi 15:4-5 that says, "Behold, I say unto you that the law is fulfilled that was given unto Moses. Behold, "I Am" he that gave the law, and I am he who covenanted with my people Israel, therefore, the law in me is fulfilled." And in 3 Nephi 20:11-17 that says, "Ye remember that I spoke unto you, and said that when the words of Isaiah should be fulfilled – behold they are written, ye have them before you, therefore search them – and verily, verily, I say unto you, that when they shall be fulfilled then is the fulfilling of the covenant which the Father hath made unto his people, O House of Israel.

Please watch on YouTube: Isaiah's Prophecy Will Be Fulfilled – New Earth Revealed, by Grace Digital Network. And then shall the remnants, which shall be scattered abroad upon the face of the earth, be gathered in from the east and from the west, and from the south and from the north; and they shall be brought to the knowledge of the Lord their God, who hath redeemed them. And the Father hath commanded me that I should give unto you this land, for your inheritance. And I say unto you, that if the Gentiles do not repent after the blessing which they shall receive, after they have scattered my people – then shall ye, who are a remnant of the House of Jacob, go forth among them; and ye shall be in the midst of them who shall be many; and ye shall be among them as a lion among the beasts of the forest, and as a young lion among the flocks of sheep, who, if he goeth through both treadeth down and teareth in pieces, and none can deliver. Thy hand shall be lifted up upon thine adversaries, and all thine enemies shall be cut off." Please continue to read up to verse forty-six. The Messiah took away the Law of Moses, but He didn't leave us lawless instead He gave us a New Law – His Commandments and instituted the ordinance of the sacrament – a holy priesthood ordinance that helps remind us of the Savior's Atonement and during the sacrament, we partake in breaking of bread and the drinking of wine. We do this in remembrance of His flesh and His blood, which He gave as a sacrifice for us and as we partake of the sacrament, which we renew our sacred covenants with the Heavenly Father.

However, the spirit of the Law of Moses; is still valid today as much as it ever was in the beginning when it was given a spiritual theocratic government that existed until the fullness of the gospel. And the main reason we should read the Book of Mormon, regardless that it was given to the Gentiles, is because it's true evidence of the Messiah and His Gospel of Grace, making this book a witness to the Holy Bible. Even Ezekiel's prophecy literally and figuratively said that the two sticks or the two books will become one testimony of the principles of the gospel of the Messiah. The gospel has almost reached the four corners of the earth but not yet: There are still a very few remote areas in the world that the gospel has not been preached only because of the language barriers. What's happening in today's society is a reminder of a quote from Elder D. Todd Christofferson, - a religious leader and a former lawyer and he said, "Sustainability is not guaranteed, especially for a thriving society because it can fall at any time when it abandons the cardinal virtues that uphold it peace and prosperity." A lot of people are curious about this question: Is America in the Bible? The answer is yes! According to the NIV Quiet Time Bible in Daniel 2:42-45 says, "As the toes were partly iron and partly clay, so this kingdom will be partly strong and partly brittle. And just as you saw the iron mixed with baked clay, so the people will be a mixture and will not remain united any more than iron mixes with clay. In the time of those kings, the God of heaven will set up a kingdom that will never be destroyed, nor will it be left to another people. It will crush all those kingdoms and bring them to an end, but it will itself endure forever.

This is the meaning of the vision of the rock cut out of a mountain, but not by human hands – a rock that broke the iron, the bronze, the clay, the silver and the gold to pieces. The great God has shown the king what will take place in the future. The dream is true, and the interpretation is trustworthy." Spiritually, the only thing that is left of the statue of King Nebuchadnezzar, is both ankles and both feet that represent the last kingdoms on earth however we are just waiting on that rock from heaven to destroy the rest of the statue: Meaning God himself is going to set up His eternal kingdom on earth, this is the prophecy that foretold by Daniel to King Nebuchadnezzar, about the coming future kingdom outside of time and space. And in Matthew 24:14, that says, "And this gospel of the Kingdom will be preached in the whole world as a testimony to all nations and then the end will come." From earning our independence in 1776 to 2024, which is only 248 years – America is a young nation compared to the other nation's timeline. People or tribes have lived on this land for at least 15,000 years or longer before the Europeans arrived here, according to the Book of Mormon. I remember a particular pastor told me that the skin color of the characters that's in the Bible are not important, which is false! The skin color of characters in the Bible represent certain people, with certain promises, which can help identify African Americans as – Hebrew's – and connecting African Americans to the Bible, as the House of Israel and the House of Judah. Even in the Book of Revelation gives a description of the Messiah, in His glory as a man of color, so why do we still believe that our Messiah is a – white man name Jesus?

The atonement of God is extended to everyone, and everybody have an opportunity to embrace eternal life, therefore it's God planned to bring the Gentiles and Jews together to make one house and that's - The House of God. The death of our Messiah, open the door for the Gentiles to be adopted into the Abrahamic Covenant, by accepting the fullness of the Gospel of Grace, as it is revealed in the Book of Mormon and in the Holy Bible.

Metaphysics

What is "Metaphysics" and how can we apply this to our spiritual life? It's the search for the reality, the opposite of perception. The search for who am I, what am I, where have I been, and where I'm going? If we can find the answers to these questions – we can find our place in society; it also acknowledges the respect of the beauty in all of God's creation, knowing the set of principles or law that was laid down by an authority as being incontrovertibly true. Laws that are not created by man, but rather explores the immutable laws of nature set by the Creator. Metaphysics is a branch of philosophy that studies the ultimate existence of reality without being bound to any one theological doctrine, which includes all religions, but transcends them all. And this is the only science that's capable of inquiring beyond physical science because the universe govern the spiritual life of earth. Spiritual Laws, plays important role in our everyday life by self-improving and personal development but allowing the Holy Spirit to merge us in the truth. The Supreme God Parmantma - is always with us in our every circumstances; whatever it is! The Spiritual Law – is a long awaiting guide to find Help or seek Help: This credible, authentic and reliable source of spiritual knowledge called: Wisdom, that provides constant guidance. The mysteries of life will guide us in the direction of finding the understanding that there is an God.

Self-fulfilling prophecy starts with believing in the Almighty Creator of Heaven and Earth. This was one of the parables that our Messiah, was trying to teach us about that if we put positive energy in the direction of the one who created energy, something is going to happen! Our thoughts is the action of our product that we can produce with the ideas of our subconscious thoughts - which is the Laws of Creation. However the opposite is true so we have to be careful with our thoughts because we don't want to create evil; which can happen! What we choose to create will apply in our life , this is called the Law of Existence: Meaning our thoughts process when meditating or prayer can sum up vibrations according to our command from our emotional center of our subconscious mind. Our Messiah informed us that the things we ask for in prayer, and in His name, will come to pass if we believe. Faith is the substance of things that we hope for, and the evidence of things that is not seen beyond the physical world and this is called – Metaphysics. So, the metaphysical goes beyond the physical world to invite an awareness of senses, facts, events, conditions and situations but we have to try and see life from more than just the physical reality. However, it teaches us that there's a huge part of power helping us deal with understanding, and some may call this the presence – God. Other may call it "Infinite Intelligence" not artificial intelligence because it's divine. And we are encouraged to explore the laws of the universe like: The Law of Abundance, The Law of Attraction, The Law of Compensation, The Law of Freedom, The Law of Life, The Law of Love, The Law of Perfection, and The Law of Truth.

Our thoughts hold spiritual power of tremendous potency but only by our thoughts we either raise ourselves up and connect with the power of the universe or cut ourselves off entirely from the divine inflow of blessing. Because our thoughts are our greatest weapon to draw from the infinite consciousness of the divine source: Which is God! It is written: In the NIV Quiet Time Bible in Matthew 6:33-34 that says, "But seek first his Kingdom and His righteousness, and all these things will be given to you as well. Therefore, do not worry about tomorrow, for tomorrow will worry about itself: Each day has enough trouble of its own." Eventually in life we will find out that all provision has already been made and our daily needs are available to us all because God is the infinite bread of life, Amen.

Remember

The second blood covenant is extended to both olive trees Jews and Gentiles, a redemption plan for the New Jerusalem and the coming Kingdom of the Messiah: It's the dispensationalism theological system of God about the coming kingdom that going to be on earth for one thousand years. Just about every major prophet that is in the Bible came from the seed of Adam's bloodline and this alone makes the character's skin color of the Bible important but today, everyone who believes in the Messiah symbolizes are the body of Him through faith, which means circumcision of the heart. This may be something that you heard before but it's truth, grace and mercy are the reason we are forgiven for our sins. So there's nothing we can do to be save but believe in the power of our Messiah: There nothing that our Messiah cannot fix either it's mentally, physically, spiritually or emotionally. Nothing beyond anyone's imagination that can stop us from being successful in life because of the order of metaphysics. We have the power to draw from the universe if we align ourselves up with the Spirit of God – the Holy Spirit. Please watch the YouTube channel called: The Holy Spirit is Female – with receipts (Lesson Starts @ 13:37). There's a lot of things that we don't know about the mystery of God; this is why we should always be open minded.

Especially when it comes down to new information and not be afraid to research, research and search for the truth then pray for what you discover because it might be the truth. Hopefully, this might give a little understanding on why I stand that the Holy Spirit is our Spiritual Mother: Please watch the YouTube channel called: Proof the Holy Spirit is Feminine (A Little Greek Lesson). God himself walked the path of the first "Blood Covenant" by smoke and fire just like He did when He led His children out of captivity centuries ago, but today it's our mind that's in captivity and still He want to lead His children out of captivity by regeneration or renewing the mind. According to the NIV Quiet Time Bible in Hebrews 9:11-15 that says, "When Christ came as high priest of the good things that are already here, he went through the greater and more perfect tabernacle that is not man-made, that is to say, not a part of this creation. He did not enter by means of the blood of goats and calves; but he entered the Most Holy Place once for all by his own blood, having obtained eternal redemption. The blood of goats and bulls and the ashes of a heifer sprinkled on those who are ceremonially unclean sanctify them so that they are outwardly clean. How much more, then, will the blood of Christ, who through the eternal Spirit offered himself unblemished to God, cleanse our consciences from acts that lead to death, so that we may serve the living God! For this reason, Christ is the mediator of a new covenant, that those who are called may receive the promised eternal inheritance – now that he has died as a ransom to set them free from the sins committed under the first covenant."

The first blood covenant is known as the "Abrahamic Covenant" which signifies the life from which the blood comes, according to Leviticus 17:11 that says, "For the life of a creature is in the blood, and I have given it to you to make atonement for yourselves on the altar; it is the blood that makes atonement for one's life." We have the "Mosaic Covenant" which is also a blood covenant that requires the blood to be sprinkled on the tabernacle, the scroll and all the people, according to Hebrews 9:19-21 that says, "When Moses had proclaimed every commandment of the law to all the people, he took the blood of calves, together with water, scarlet wool and branches of hyssop, and sprinkled the scroll and all the people. He said: This is the blood of the covenant, which God has commanded you to keep. In the same way, he sprinkled with the blood both the tabernacle, and everything used in its ceremonies." Without the shedding of blood there's no forgiveness, according to Hebrews 9:22 that says, "In fact, the law requires that nearly everything be cleansed with blood, and without the shedding of blood there is no forgiveness." All of these covenants were a shadow of a better covenant that came "The Messiah" is the new covenant of faith in Him and in the Holy Spirit. God's children have a heavenly sanctuary, according to the NIV Quiet Time Bible in Hebrews 8:1-2 that says, "The point of what we are saying is this: We do have such a high priest, who sat down at the right hand of the throne of the Majesty in heaven, and who serves in the sanctuary, the true tabernacle set up by the Lord, not by man."

And according to Colossians 2:16-23 that says, "Therefore do not let anyone judge you by what you eat or drink, or with regard to a religious festival, a New Moon celebration or a Sabbath day. These are a shadow of the things that were to come; the reality, however, is found in Christ. Do not let anyone who delights in false humility and the worship of angels disqualify you for the prize. Such a person goes into great detail about what he has seen, and his unspiritual mind puffs him up with idle notions. He has lost connection with the Head, from whom the whole body, supported and held together by its ligaments and sinews, grows as God causes it to grow. Since you died with Christ to the basic principles of this world, why, as though you still belonged to it, do you submit to its rules: Do not handle! Do not taste! Do not touch! These are all destined to perish with use, because they are based on human commands and teachings. Such regulations indeed have an appearance of wisdom, with their self-imposed worship, their false humility and their harsh treatment of the body, but they lack any value in restraining sensual indulgence." Also according to the NIV Quiet Time Bible in 1 Peter 4:16-19 that says, "However, if you suffer as a Christian, do not be ashamed, but praise God that you bear that name: For it is time for judgment to begin with the family of God; and if it begins with us, what will the out-come be for those who do not obey the gospel of God? And, if it is hard for the righteous to be saved, what will become of the ungodly and the sinner? So then, those who suffer according to God's will should commit themselves to their faithful Creator and continue to do good."

It our responsibility to pray and search the Scripture for the truth, of who we are, and who we are not! Yes, we have an responsibility to our country but the point of what I'm saying is this: The closing of the door is not by man hand but God, like in Noah days, he continued to preach to the people until the door of the ark was closed by the hand of God. Observing the Gospel of Grace is a call for God's children to enter into a place of refuge or shelter. According to 2 Chronicles 30:6-9 that says, "At the king's command, couriers went throughout Israel and Judah with letters from the king and from his officials, which read: People of Israel, return to the LORD, the God of Abraham, Isaac and Jacob, that he may return to you who are left, who have escaped from the hand of the kings of Assyria. Do not be like your fathers and brothers, who were unfaithful to the LORD, the God of their fathers, so that he made them an object of horror, as you see. Do not be stiff-necked, as your fathers were; submit to the LORD. Come to the sanctuary, which he has consecrated forever. Serve the LORD your God, so that his fierce anger will turn away from you. If you return to the LORD, then your brothers and your children will be shown compassion by their captors and will come back to this land, for the LORD your God is gracious and compassionate. He will not turn his face from you if you return to him." This is evidence that our body today represent the Spiritual Tabernacle; the same one that Moses and King Solomon built here on earth, starting with the altar where the priest sacrificed the lamb which represents the "Cross" as believers we supposed to wear our cross around our neck to remind us to always do good.

It was our Messiah's blood that was sprinkled on the Mercy Seat, or the Ark of the Covenant. The "Labor" or the washing of the hands that represent baptism; this is where our name enters into the Book of Life. The "Showbread" represents the Word of God: According to the NIV Quiet Time Bible in Matthew 4:4 that says, "The Messiah answered, it is written: Man does not live on bread alone, but on every word that comes from the mouth of God." So, how often do you read our Bible? Our strength comes by reading and hearing the Word of God. The "Altar of Incense" is the prayers of God's children, Jew and Gentiles; praises go up and blessings come down. The "Candlestick" represents being a witness for God – the light in the world that is full of darkness, especially when dealing with adversity. The "Veil" that was torn in half represents our Messiah's skin – when His skin was torn by the beating He took from the Roman soldiers, now the Heavenly Sanctuary is open to all who believe that "He Is" the Son of God – the Messiah, our Savior, and our Spiritual Brother: That died and went to Hell, to defeated Satan for the lost souls that he had in captivity, tormenting them until our Savior led them out into paradise for the "Second Pass Over" so now when we die; we either rest in our grave, or enter into paradise to wait for the final gathering and for the one thousand year of rest with the Messiah. It's our Messiah that has the keys to the gates of hell and everyone who is going to enter into hell is on the authority of the Messiah, which will soon be the lake of fire.

Wallace Stanciel

When we hear about people having a dream or a near death experience meeting the Messiah, either in paradise or at the gates of hell sometimes we are given a second chance to become a better person because of Mercy and Grace. According to the NIV Quiet Time Bible in Luke 16:19-31 that says, "There was a rich man who was dressed in purple and fine lined and lived in luxury every day: At his gate was laid a beggar named Lazarus, covered with sores and longing to eat what fell from the rich man's table. Even the dogs came and licked his sores. The time came when the beggar died, and the angels carried him to Abraham's side. The rich man also died and was buried. In hell, where he was in torment, he looked up and saw Abraham far away, with Lazarus by his side. So, he called to him, Father Abraham, have pity on me and send Lazarus to dip the tip of his finger in water and cool my tongue, because I am in agony in this fire. But Abraham replied, "Son, remember that in your lifetime you received your good things, while Lazarus received bad things, but now he is comforted here, and you are in agony. And besides all this, between us and you a great chasm has been fixed, so that those who want to go from here to you cannot, nor can anyone cross over from there to us. He answered, then I beg you, father, send Lazarus to my father's house, for I have five brothers. Let him warn them, so that they will not also come to this place of torment.

Abraham replied, "They have Moses and the Prophets; let them listen to them. "No, Father Abraham," he said, but if someone from the dead goes to them, they will repent. He said to him, if they do not listen to Moses and the Prophets, they will not be convinced even if someone rise from the dead." And in Revelation 20:14-15 that says, "Then death and Hades were thrown into the lake of fire. The lake of fire is the second death. If anyone's name was not found written in the book of life, he(she) was thrown into the lake of fire." Therefore, not too many pastors going to teach on the subject that hell, is out of business and the new owner is the Messiah. Also that are not going teach that the Holy Spirit; is a – woman! Because it's goes against the standard of Christianity - this religious system is trying to keep the believer mind in a box and if we want to escape from that box; we have to read Spiritual Scripture outside the King James Bible. For example: It was even influenced by modern Protestants, such as John Wesley, who concluded that in the image of the Holy Spirit as a woman or a mother, one may attain a better appreciation of the fullness of the divine – Trinity. In Jewish theology, divine wisdom is a central concept of Proverbs 8 - suggesting that wisdom existed for ages before God's creation of the world. The Hebrew word for wisdom is "hokmah" grammatically feminine and thus can be personified as a – woman. This has led scholars to believe that wisdom referenced in the Book Proverbs is a female – the Holy Spirit or the Holy Mother of creation.

And according to Genesis 5:1-2, when God created mankind, He made them in the likeness of God's. He created them male and female and blessed them and He named them "Mankind" when they were created, but some scholars interpret Genesis, to mean that God made woman from the image of man but Thomas Aquinas wrote: In a primary sense, God's image in woman is found in man as in woman as regards that in which the idea of image principally consists, namely an intelligent nature *(Wisdom)*. But in a secondary sense, God's image is found in man in a way in which it is not found in woman; for man is the beginning and end of woman, just as God is the beginning and end of creation. And this is why marriage is so important according to Augustine of Hippo and on the Trinity: The woman together with her own husband is the image of God, so that the whole substance may be one image; but when she is referred separately to her quality of help-meet, which regards the woman herself alone, then she is not the image of God; but as regards the man alone, he is the image of God as fully and completely as when the woman is joined with him in one. Though it may appear this issue only matters to academics and theologians, the quandary is still debated in modern times however, in 1999, the Methodist Church in England introduced a new prayer book that references God as "Our Father and Our Mother" Reverend Neil Dixon, the church's head of liturgy at the time, explained.

Exclusively male imagery doesn't really do justice to God, and if it is an article of our religion that human beings are made in the image of God, then both male and female must help us to understand God's nature and express our understanding of God's nature, and according to Reverend Dixon, we're following a Christian tradition of using female images in reference to God; which is evident in the Bible. Some evidence can take us out of our comfort zone because of tradition and the topic about woman pastors make other male pastors uncomfortable, so what is the proper leadership role for the women in today churches? But there's a major dispute or concern going on that addressing woman in the 21st century, especially on abortion. With Roe v. Wade overturned by the Supreme Court, each state has the right to control its level of access to abortion or ban it completely. Legal chaos has erupted: Though many state legislatures are in session, courts and state executives are sorting through trigger laws about abortion bans. The number of states where abortion is legal are changing by the day. Published: In May 25, 2022 – Health Reporter – Shefali Luthra, with federal abortion protections likely to be struck down over the coming years, anti-abortion lawmakers are turning their attention to the next target; birth control in particular, emergency contraception and intrauterine devices (IUDs). The talks are still in their early stages but days after the leak of a draft Supreme Court decision overturning Roe v. Wade, Brent Crane, a senior state lawmaker in Idaho, said publicly he wanted to hold a hearing on banning emergency contraception.

Earlier the month, Louisiana lawmakers considered a bill that would have classified abortion as homicide – and experts said, that they might criminalized IUDs and emergency contraception as well – but the Louisiana bill ultimately failed. Mr. Ryan Peterson, the author of the book called: "The Final Nephilim" will help readers to get an understanding of what it was like in the days of Noah. But his first book is called: The Judgment of the Nephilim. Mr. Peterson gives us a good understanding of the Book of Genesis -starting at Chapter 6, so with the increase of UFOs are we about to repeat the days of Noah? With the mixing of genetics (DNA)? According to the NIV Quiet Time Bible in Genesis 6:4 that says, "The Nephilim were on the earth in those days – and also afterward – when the sons of God went to the daughters of men and had children by them: They were the heroes of old, men of renown." More and more scientists are finding that the only differences that set people apart are cultural, not racial. However, some even say that the word "race" should be abandoned because it's meaningless. Dr. Craig Venter, the head of the Celera Genomics Corporation in Rockville, Maryland, and other scientists at the National Institutes of Health – recently announced that they put together a draft of the entire sequence of the human genome. The researchers unanimously declared there is only one race: The human race. The Book of Genesis is about the Creation of God: God is commanding his children on what and what not to do! However, the fall of mankind was about the mixing of DNA because how can a woman eat a fruit and get pregnant? There's so much that we do not know!

Deliberation

The definition of "De-lib-er-a-tion" is a long and careful consideration or discussion. The three stages of deliberation process are orientation, open conflict and reconciliation. And the guideline for successful deliberation is to listen, to understand, not misrepresent other's opinions or information, focus on the heart of the discussion, identify possible realistic options for judgment, and move toward a choice. Contemplating the pros and cons of a required decision – is an often-observed activity in the process of decision making and response selection, so how long is too long on deciding for – Reparation for Black American? The National African American Reparations Commission – preliminary 10-point reparations program is a document for review, revision and adoption as a platform to guide and to struggle for reparations for people of African descent in the U.S., also for more information you can sign up and stay informed on their website. African American history in this country started with Slavery then Jim Crow laws, then criminalization, incarceration is another form of slavery, racial inequality and racial disparities all of this is a part of Black history in America. Please watch the documentary called: 13th – Directed by Ava DuVernay, this thought-provoking documentary highlights scholars, activists and politicians who analyze the criminalization of African Americans in the U.S. prison boom.

African American are the descendants of Negro Christian Slaves; and for centuries we have been chasing our true identity so the question we have to ask ourselves is this: Who are we, where, when did we originate? Another important documentary to watch is called: Black History, Black Freedom and Black Love. There are eleven episodes with icons like – Angela Davis, Jelani Cobb, Kimberle Williams Crenshaw, Nikole Hannah-Jones, Sherrilyn Ifill, John McWhorter and Cornel West: These icons give a master class on Black History, here in America. Black liberation movement which is a part of Black America History. Our Black leaders gave their life and their family life in order for Black people to have what we have in the 21st century which is: Opportunity! So do some member of the Africa American community take upon themselves the rights to take opportunity away from other member of the same race? Because we are still suffering from the mental trauma from slavery and religiously suffering from the truth of who we are! And also we suffering from mental illness of self-ownership of spiritual awareness that came from psychological trauma from hardship just by living in America. According to the NIV Quiet Time Bible in Isaiah 41:10-14 that says, "So do not fear, for I am with you: Do not be dismayed, for I am your God. I will strengthen you and help you; I will uphold you with my righteous right hand. All who rage against you will surely be ashamed and disgraced; those who oppose you will be as nothing and perish. Though you search for your enemies, you will not find them. Those who wage war against you will be like nothing at all.

For I am Almighty God, your protector who takes hold of your right hand and says to you, do not fear; I will help you. Do not be afraid, O worm Jacob, O little Israel, for I myself will help you, declares God the Almighty, your redeemer, the Holy One of Israel." The Black American communities have been inflicted with racial disparities from generation after generation in the name of "Imperialism" by gaining political, economic and religion control over Black and Brown citizens. Now the question is? Can imperialism be considered a criminal act? And can we hold these President's accountable for destroying the Black Communities: President Richard Nixon, President Ronald Reagan along with his wife Nancy Reagan "Just Say No to Drugs" and President Bill Clinton, for committing a hate crime in the Black and Brown communities with their policies like; War on Crime, War on Drugs, and The Three Strikes you're out incarcerated for life or a very long time! It's was policies like these that damage the Black and Brown communities also families, so again the question is asked! Is imperialism the law of rights or is it the law of the mighty, or is it just hypocritical to assume a person is guilty because the color of their skin? America has one flag that everyone pledged allegiance to, so, why are so mamy people are still trying to fly two flags? Dr. Martin Luther King Jr. was for reparation because when he recognized what our ancestors contributed economically to making this nation great: He stated to campaign a second march on Washington D.C., and maybe this was one of the reason that he was assassinated: Because he started to talk about – Money! Reparation is more than money; it's about identity.

103

More than thirteen million Black people that were being transported to this country for slavery died during the journey to this country, however this was imperialism in action. Even though today in 2024, President Joe Biden executed an executive order around racial equity starting with the first Black and Asian female Vice President – Kamala Harris and his cabinet members are the most racially and gender diverse picks in American history. Another documentary to watch is called: Heavy is the Crown, it's a three parts series with Professor James Small – Part 1: Indigenous Americans, Malcolm X, & 2Pac. Part 2: Ancient Kemet, Coptic Church, & The Slave Trade. Part 3: The Trinity, Matriarchy, & The Attack on the Black Family. His interview is an eye-opening topic on Black History; and it gives important evidence of what led to - Imperialism. Maybe this will give an understanding or insight about who we are, and how it feel being Black in America. According to the NIV Quiet Time Bible in Romans 3:23-31 that says, "There is no difference, for all have sinned and fall short of the glory of God and are justified freely by his grace through the redemption that came by Christ Jesus. God presented him as a sacrifice of atonement, through faith in his blood. He did this to demonstrate his justice, because in his forbearance he had left the sins committed beforehand unpunished – he did it to demonstrate his justice at the present time, so as to be just and the one who justifies those who have faith in Jesus. Where, then, is boasting? It is excluded: On what principle? On that of observing the law? No, but on that of faith. For we maintain that a man is justified by faith apart from observing the law. Is God the God of Jew only?

Is he not the God of Gentiles too? Yes, of Gentiles too, since there is only one God, who will justify the circumcised by faith and the uncircumcised through that same faith. Do we then nullify the law by this faith? Not at all! Rather, we uphold   the   law."

CHAPTER ONE
The Kingdom Message

T he "Kingdom Message" is the Gospel of Grace, which the New Testament - announcing about the good news of a – Coming Kingdom on earth or a New Government with a King – our High Priest over the Temple of God. According to the NIV Quiet Time Bible in Daniel 2:44 that says, "In the time of those kings, the God of heaven; will set up a kingdom that will never be destroyed, nor will it be left to another people. It will crush all those kingdoms and bring them to an end, but it will self-endure forever." The late great Dr. Myles Munroe, is an expert on the subject of the Kingdom Message: We can find his teaching on – YouTube channel called: The Kingdom of God Defined, Kingdom Theology of the Bible, The Practical Approach to Seeking the Kingdom of God, The Kingdom Principles of the Keys – Parts 1, 2, and 3, The Keys to Accessing the Things of the Kingdom, and there's more teaching about the kingdom message that can strengthen our relationship with God. And by using emotional intelligence which is defined by four attributes; self-management, self-awareness, social awareness, and relationship management plus these are essential skills that we need that can give us the ability to walk and talk with the Spirit of God.

Emotional awareness helps with decision making when it comes down to controlling our emotions, which can give people a chance to think before reacting to an issue or situation or making a decision. This is where emotional awareness comes into play and if we are willing to listen, the Holy Spirit is ready to help us with our decision through subconscious, which create self-awareness. According to the NIV Quiet Time Bible in Psalm 121:1-8 that says, "I lift up my eyes to the hills – where does my help come from? My help comes from the LORD, the maker of heaven and earth. He will not let your foot slip – He who watches over you will not slumber; indeed, He who watches over Israel will neither slumber nor sleep. The LORD watches over you – the LORD is your shade at your right hand; the sun will not harm you by day, nor the moon by night. The LORD will keep you from all harm – He will watch over your life; the LORD will watch over your coming and going both now and forevermore." Understanding the Kingdom Message – so is important according to Luke 4:42-43 that says, "At daybreak Christ went out to a solitary place the people were looking for him and when they came to where he was, they tried to keep him from leaving them. But he said, I must preach the Good News of the Coming Kingdom of God to the other towns also, because that is why I was sent." The testimony of the New Testament is unanimous about the Kingdom Message of the coming Kingdom of God on earth; this is the message that was at the heart of the Messiah. So, why are the pastors of today's churches not preaching or teaching this message? Why?

They teach and preach about the pagan holidays like Christmas and Easter, however they have no problem allowing the devil hand to play a significant role in the churches, and as believers, some people don't even see it! But if we want to truly understand the Kingdom Message, we have to asked ourselves what make this message so important, according to the Book of Isaiah 9:6-7 that says, "For to us a child is born, to us a Son is given, and the government will be on his shoulders. And he will be called Wonderful - Counselor, Mighty God, Everlasting Father, Prince of Peace: Of the increase of his government and peace there will be no end. He will reign on David's throne and over His Kingdom, establishing and upholding it with justice and righteousness from time on and forever. The zeal of the LORD Almighty will accomplish this." King David ruled over a real kingdom in Jerusalem, and that very same kingdom is the one our Messiah will be ruling over on earth and He will sit in that very same chair ruling over the earth and His kingdom will be called: New Jerusalem. According to the NIV Quiet Time Bible in Revelation 19:16 that says, "On his robe and on his thigh, he has the name written: King of King and Lord of Lord." And in Revelation 20:6-10 that say, "Blessed and holy are those who have part in the first resurrection: The second death has no power over them, but they will be priests of God and of Christ and will reign with him for a thousand years. When the thousand years are over, Satan will be released from his prison and will go out to deceive the nations in the four corners of the earth – Gog and Magog – to gather them for battle. In number they are like the sand on the seashore.

They marched across the breadth of the earth and surrounded the camp of God's people, the city he loves. But fire came down from heaven and devoured them. And the devil, who deceived them, was thrown into the lake of burning sulfur, where the beast and the false prophet had been thrown. They will be tormented day and night for ever and ever." Some believers go to church every Sunday and their pastor never preach out of the Book of Revelation, which is a part of the Kingdom Message: And we go about our day believing that perception is reality which is nothing but a lie - a work of the devil keeping God children confused about reality, but according to 1 Corinthians 14:33 that says, "For God is not a God of disorder but of peace." In the scripture, peace involves not only the end of hostilities, but the setting of things in their right order! In the Book of Zechariah 14:16-17 that says, "Then the survivors from all the nations that have attacked Jerusalem will go up year after year to worship the King, the LORD Almighty, and to celebrate the Feast of Tabernacles: If any of the peoples of the earth do not go up to (New) Jerusalem to worship the King, the LORD Almighty, they will have no rain." This is the mystery of the Kingdom Message; the role that salvation plays is the good news of the Gospel of Grace. According to the NIV Quiet Time Bible in 1 Peter 1:18-23 that says, "For you know that it was not with perishable things such as silver or gold that you were redeemed from the empty way of life handed down to you from your forefathers.

But with the precious blood of Christ, a lamb without blemish or defect. He was chosen before the creation of the world but was revealed in these last times for your sake. Through him you believe in God. Now that you have purified yourselves by obeying the truth so that you have sincere love for your brothers, love one another deeply, from the heart. For you have been born again not perishable seed but of imperishable, through the living and enduring word of God." It was nothing but the blood of the Messiah that took away the sins of the world and the sins of our forefathers: Reconciliation - means restoration of friendly relations particularly between the father and his children, according to Colossians 1:19-20 that says, "For God was pleased to have all his fullness dwell in him, and through him to reconcile to himself all things, whether things on earth or things in heaven, by making peace through his blood shed on the cross." This is the Gospel of Grace! This is the Kingdom Message!

Please watch the YouTube channel called: The Metaphysics of Time, Space and Dimensions; pt. 1, 2, and 3 plus there's also four more videos that's mind blowing and educational.

CHAPTER TWO
The Truth Un-Edited About The Days of Noah And The Great Gathering

Most people know the important of the Nation of Israel, because the Bible speaks about its biblical history according to the NIV Quiet Time Bible in Psalm 119:105 that says, "Your word is a lamp to my feet and a light for my path. I have taken an oath and confirmed that I will follow your righteous laws. I have suffered much; preserve my life, O LORD, according to your word. Accept, O LORD, the willing praise of my mouth, and teach me your laws. Though I constantly take my life in my hands; I will not forget your laws, the wicked have set a snare for me, but I have not strayed from your precepts. Your statutes are my heritage forever; they are the joy of my heart. My heart is set on keeping your decrees to the very end." But what going on right now in the land of Israel, is leading up to the Great Gathering, and the tribulation according to the Biblical conflicts that we see like; wars and rumors of wars. Throughout the history of the land Israel, this nation has always been in wars with the Philistines, Egyptians, Midianites, Moabites, Amalekites, Ammonites, the Babylonians, the Assyrians, Persians and the Romans, who crucify the Messiah.

Then came the "Hitler" again with the Assyria, Palestinian, and Hamas but the persecution of Israel, today it's only going to get worse behind every war there are demonic spirits in position to show themselves. It's hard to understand this, however, behind every war there is a demonic spirit that's leading up to the physical realm according to Ephesians 6:10-12 that says, "Finally, be strong in the Lord and in his mighty power. Put on the full armor of God so that you can take your stand against the devil's schemes. For our struggle is not against flesh and blood, but against the rulers, against the authorities, against the powers of this dark world and against the spiritual forces of evil in the heavenly realms." We live in a realm called: "Metaphysics" but we don't understand what we don't see which is the spiritual realm. According to Daniel 10:10-14, in the NIV Quiet Time Bible that says, "A hand touched me and set me trembling on my hands and knees. He said, Daniel, you who are highly esteemed, consider carefully the words I am about to say to you, and stand up, for I have now been sent to you. And when he said this to me, I stood up trembling. Then he continued: Do not be afraid, Daniel, since the first day that you set your mind to gain understanding and to humble yourself before your God, your words were heard, and I have come in response to them. But the prince of the Persian kingdom resisted me twenty-one days. Then Michael, one of the chief princes, came to help me, because I was detained there with the king of Persia. Now I have come to explain to you what will happen to your people in the future, for the vision concerns a time yet to come."

Today in the 21st century God is - the God of the Nation of Israel, biblically speaking and the land that is called: Israel. He has specific plans for that land because centuries ago it was prophesized that the Messiah, would come from the tribe of Judah, and the demonic spirit tried to stop it, according to the Book of Micah 5:2 that says, "But you, Bethlehem Ephrathah, though you are small among the clans of Judah, out of you will come for me one who will be ruler over Israel, whose origins are from of old from ancient times." All over the Old Testament and the Book of Mormon, these two witnesses have spoked about Israel and the coming of the Messiah, and now most of the religion leaders is keeping God's children mentally confused about the Great Gathering and the one thousand years of rest with the Messiah, sitting in the seat of David as our High Priest here on earth. The Book of Mormon and the Old Testament testify to the promise of the great rest with the Messiah. The meta-narrative of the Kingdom Message, is true! And when we die; we either rest in our grave or enter into paradise waiting for the Great Gathering, standing in front of the Messian to be judged for either everlasting punishment, or partaking in the 1000 years of rest with the Messiah before His second coming. According to the Book of Hebrews 2:14-17, in the NIV Quiet Time Bible that says, "Since the children have flesh and blood, he too shared in their humanity so that by his death he might destroy him who holds the power of death – that is, the devil – and free those who all their lives were held in slavery by their fear of death.

113

For surely it is not angels he helps, but Abraham's descendants. For this reason, he had to be made like his brothers in every way, in order that he might become a merciful and faithful high priest in service to God, and that he might make atonement for the sins of the people." According to the NIV Quiet Time Bible in Jeremiah 30:1-11 that says, "This is the word that came to Jeremiah from the LORD: This is what the LORD, the God of Israel, says: Write in a book all the words I have spoken to you. The days are coming, declares the LORD, when I will bring my people Israel and Judah back from captivity and restore them to the "Land" I gave their forefathers to possess, says the LORD. These are the words the LORD spoke concerning Israel and Judah: This is what the LORD says: Cries of fear are heard – terror, not peace. Ask and see; can a man bear children? Then why do I see every strong man with his hands on his stomach like a woman in labor, every face turned deathly pale? How awful that day will be! None will be like it. It will be a time of trouble for Jacob, but he will be saved out of it. In that day, declares the LORD Almighty, I will break the yoke off their necks and will tear off their bonds; no longer will foreigners enslave them. Instead, they will raise up for them. So do not fear, O Jacob my servant; do not be dismayed, O Israel, declares the LORD. I will surely save you out of a distant place, your descendants from the land of their exile. Jacob will again have peace and security, and no one will make him afraid. I am with you and will save you, declares the LORD.

Though I completely destroy all the nations among which I scatter you, I will not completely destroy you. I will discipline you, but only with justice; I will not let you go entirely unpunished. Therefore, the time that we are living in is scary, because the third temple is about to be rebuilt meaning; the antichrist is going to try to sit in the seat of the High Priest which belong to the Messiah, according to the Book of 2 Thessalonians 2:1-4 that says, "Concerning the coming of our Lord Jesus Christ and our being gathered to him, we ask you, brothers, not to become easily unsettled or alarmed by some prophecy, report of letter supposed to have come from us, saying that the day of the Lord has already come. Don't let anyone deceive you in any way, for, that day will not come, until the rebellion occurs, and the man of lawlessness is revealed, the man doomed to destruction. He will oppose and will exalt himself over everything that is called God or is worshiped, so that he sets himself up in God's temple, proclaiming himself to be God." And then it will be a terrible time for the people of Israel and the world, according to the Book of Daniel 8:25 that says, "He will cause deceit to prosper, and he will consider himself superior. When they feel secure, he will destroy many and take his stand against the Prince of Princes: Yet he will be destroyed, but not by human power." In the Book of Matthew 24:29-31 that says, "Immediately after the distress of those days the sun will be darkened, and the moon will not give its light; the stars will fall from the sky, and the heavenly bodies will be shaken.

115

At that time, the sign of the Son of Man will appear in the sky, and the nations of the earth will mourn. They will see the Son of Man coming on the clouds of the sky, with power and great glory. And he will send his angels with a loud trumpet call, and they will gather his elect from the four winds, from one end of the heavens of the other." But what about the "Two Witnesses" according to the NIV Quiet Time Bible in Revelation 11:4 that says, "These are the two olive trees and the two lampstands that stand before the Lord of the earth." And in Deuteronomy 19:15 that says, "One witness is not enough to convict a man accused of any crime of offense he may have committed. A matter must be established by the testimony of two or three witnesses." However, the two witnesses must appear after the "Great Gathering" of God's children even though some people think that it might be the spirit of Moses and the spirit of Elijah or the spirit of Enoch and the spirit of Elijah because they didn't die. But according to the Book of Mark 9:13 that says, "But I tell you, Elijah has come, and they have done to him everything they wished, just as it is written about him." Remember, Satan fought the Arch-Angel Michael over the body of Moses, because Satan accused Moses of sinning at Meribah, claiming that he has the rights to Moses body, reminding God - that you commanded Moses to speak to the rock at Meribah but instead, Moses struck the rock with his staff, according to the Book of Numbers 20:10-13.

And in Luke 24:1-8 also in Acts 1:10-11; the two witnesses appeared. So the question is? Has the two witnesses already arrived? In the New Testament a significant event took place the – transfiguration of the Messiah, and with him were the two witnesses that appeared in their glory "Moses and Elijah" in their resurrected bodies, it is recorded in all three of Synoptic Gospels: Mark 9:2-13, Matthew 17:1-13 and Luke 9:28-36. Then again, can it be the Gentiles and the Jews; are these the two olive trees which is the two witnesses, because they have been witnesses to the world for over 2,000 years but still the fulfillment of the Gentiles is not complete. According to the Book of Jeremiah 11:16 that says, "The LORD called you a thriving olive tree with fruit beautiful in form. But with the roar of a mighty storm, he will set it on fire and its branches will be broken." The stories of the Bible has already been told and we're living in the future of what was told about the two olive tree, however we're just playing our parts and waiting for the concluding, according to the NIV Quiet Time Bible in Isaiah 43:10-13 that says, "You are my witnesses, declares the LORD, and my servant whom I have chosen, so that you may know and believe me and understand that I am He. Before me, no God was formed, nor will there be one after me. I, even I, am the LORD, and apart from me there is no savior, I have revealed, saved, and proclaimed – I, and not some foreign god among you. You are my witnesses, declares the LORD, that I am God."

117

And in Isaiah 44:8 that says, "Do not tremble, do not be afraid. Did I not proclaim this and foretell it long ago? You are my witnesses. Is there any God besides me? No, there is no other Rock: I know not one." The "Word of God" both the Old Testament and the New Testament, must be fulfilled and all things have to be restored so what has been scattered is about to be gathered. To get help with understanding of the Book of Revelation, please check out this amazing book by Nelson Walters called: Revelation Deciphered; it's a fantastic contribution to the study of the Book of Revelation. This book is like nothing you will ever read before concerning the great gathering with precision.

CHAPTER THREE
Distractions

A distraction is something that turns our attention away from something that we should be concentrate on, and when everything that's happening in the world our focus should be on God. But how can we do this when everybody and everything around us seem to be a perception. People lying about who they are or just lying for no reason at all, according to the NIV Quiet Time Bible in John 8:44 that says, "You belong to your father, the devil, and you want to carry out your father's desire. He was a murderer from the beginning, not holding on to the truth, for there is no truth in him. When he lies, he speaks his native language, for he is a liar and the father of lies." And the bad thing about the devil, he will use anyone to distract you from the plan that God has for your life, your purpose or your destiny. He will place a demon in a person to block your blessing or to rob you from your blessing; he will used your girlfriend/wife or boyfriend/husband to betrayed you, a family member that will verbally abuse you to distract you from your purpose, or make your boss at work past you over for promotion, or co-worker to sell you out for whatever reason, or make your close friends betray you by using his demons called: Jealousy and Envy.

And the thing about the devil - at any cost he will set booby traps to kill, steal, and destroy a person life. However, the thing about all of this; some of the peole he will send are not our enemy – it's the devil at work that's adding distractions to our life. According to the Book of Ephesians 6:12 that says, "For our struggle is not against flesh and blood, but against the rulers, against the authorities, against the powers of this dark world and against the spiritual forces of evil in the heavenly realms." The real reality is "Metaphysics" we're living in both physical and a spiritual realms of this world, and the devil is at war behind the scenes in the spiritual realm trying his best to destroy God children. According to the NIV Quiet Time Bible in Matthew 16:21-23 that says, "From that time on Jesus began to explain to his disciples that he must go to Jerusalem and suffer many things at the hands of the elders, chief priests and teachers of the law, and that he must be killed and on the third day be raised to life. Peter took him aside and began to rebuke him, never, Lord! He said. This shall never happen to you! Jesus turned and said to Peter, get behind me, Satan! You are a stumbling block to me; you do not have in mind the things of God, but the things of men." The point is this! Jesus did not get mad at Peter but recognize who was behind Peter thoughts. Today, we are distracted by many things around our personal life and what we see and hear on the news like wars, rumors of wars, the economy, political corruption, and wickedness is just the order of the day.

The world is changing right in front of our face especially when innocent people are being treated like criminals, marriages are falling apart, diseases are taking their tolls on the population and all of these things can be overwhelming therefore we must keep our focus on God before the situation of life get out of control. According to the NIV Quiet Time Bible in John 16:33 that says, "I have told you these things, so that in me you may have peace. In this world you will have trouble. But take heart! I have overcome the world." And Matthew 24:6-8 that says, "You will hear of wars and rumors of wars but see to it that you are not alarmed. Such things must happen, but the end is still to come. Nation will rise against nation, and kingdom against kingdom. There will be famines and earthquakes in various places. All these are the beginning of birth pains." When people attack God's children with malice, jealousy and envy as believers, we should not attack with the same negative energy; I know this sounds a little crazy, but we must pray for them because they're trespassing in our life's. And the hard part is to become a peacemakers of our own emotions, this is called – Emotional Intelligence, the same tactics the Dr. Martin Luther King Jr., used to led a non-violent peace protest, according to the NIV Quiet Time Bible in Romans 12:1-21 that says, "Therefore, I urge you, brothers, in view of God's mercy, to offer your body as (a) living sacrifices, holy and pleasing to God – this is your spiritual act of worship. Do not conform any longer to the pattern of this world but be transformed by the renewing of your mind. Then you will be able to test and approve what God's will is – His good, pleasing and perfect will.

For by the grace given me I say to every one of you: Do not think of yourself more highly than you ought, but rather think of yourself with sober judgment, in accordance with the measure of faith God has given you. Just as each of us has one body with many members and these members do not all have the same function, so in Christ, we who are many form one body, and each member belongs to all the others. We have different gifts, according to the grace given us. If a man's gift is prophesying, let him use it in proportion to his faith. If it is serving, let him serve; if it is teaching, let him teach; if it is encouraging, let him encourage; if it is contributing to the needs of others, let him give generously; if it is leadership, let him govern diligently; if it is showing mercy, let him do it cheerfully. Love must be sincere. Hate what is evil; cling to what is good. Be devoted to one another in brotherly love. Honor one another above yourselves. Never be lacking in zeal, but keep your spiritual fervor, serving God. Be joyful in hope, patient in affliction, faithful in prayer. Share with God's people who are in need. Practice hospitality. Bless those who persecute you; bless and do not curse. Rejoice with those who rejoice, mourn with those who mourn. Live in harmony with one another. Do not be proud but be willing to associate with people of low position. Do not be conceited. Do not repay anyone evil for evil. Be careful to do what is right in the eyes of everybody. If it is possible, as far as it depends on you, live at peace with everyone.

Do not take revenge, my friends, but leave room for God's wrath, for it is written: It is mine to revenge, I will repay, says God. On the contrary, if your enemy is hungry, feed him, if he is thirsty, give him something to drink. In doing this, you will heap burning coals on his head. Do not be overcome by evil, but overcome evil with good." Renewing our mind can eliminate distraction but it takes dedication of oneself daily, it's not just a one-time thing because withdrawing from worldly trends is an act of obedient according to the Book of Galatians 5:21 that says, "The acts of the sinful nature are obvious, sexual immorality, impurity and debauchery, idolatry and witchcraft; hatred, discord, jealousy, fits of rage, selfish ambition, dissension, factions and envy; drunkenness, orgies, and the like. I warn, as I did before, that those who live like this will not inherit the Kingdom of God." Jealousy and envy drag destruction they are two of the toughest evil spirits we will come up against in our lives, because it stems from a place in the heart, as painful it may seem, jealousy and envy are common human feelings. It can be that the devil is working on our emotions, however, jealousy and envy travel together they are still the cause of most conflicts in leadership and in our personal lives. There will always be people with more talents, in better shape health wise, have more money or have a better reputation than others. Entitlement is a myth, it doesn't help to think that someone deserves better than someone else just because – this can easily lead into ignorance, hating and greed.

And we all know that hate arises from ignorance and greed arises from the heart. Controlling our thoughts can be difficult but not impossible, it's our thoughts that control our emotions and this is why we should renew our mind daily. Because it's our mind that's control our life whatever happens in our life starts from our mind. And everything starts with a decision so what are we thinking about? As parents we should be saying this to our children: Watch your thoughts, they will become your words, watch your words, they will become your actions, watch your actions, they will become your habits, watch your habits, they will become your character, watch your character, it will become your destiny. Distractions is everywhere but one thing that a marathon runner do; they always set their hearts and minds on finishing the race. According to the NIV Quiet Time Bible in Colossians 3:1-4 that says, "Since, then you have been raised with Christ, set your hearts on things above, where Christ is seated at the right hand of God. Set your minds on things above, not on earthly things: For you died, and your life is now hidden with Christ in God. When Christ, who is your life, appears, then you also will appear with him in glory." We cannot let distractions get the best of us; our focus should be on the next step or the chapter in our life until the race is complete. If we have to shed friends, family member, lose jobs or anything else that might slow us down from living a Christian life, get back in the race because you're not at the finish line. In church, why do we have distractions? Or should I dare to say; why do we have so many distractions? Is it because the truth is under attack? Or can we blame the ones that's giving the message?

What is: Perspicuity of Scripture? Clarity: Affirms that scripture is able to be understood rightly, not that it will always be understood rightly. And the Word of God should be clear about everything that is necessary for His children to obeyed in order to live a save life. So, the question must be asked: Why are there so many people leave out of church service, not even knowing or caring what the preacher just preached about? And who or what, can we blame? If to say, that something is perspicacious, meaning that it's clear and understandable, why do so many Christians act ungodly? And the ones that's trying their best to act godly; why are they constantly under spiritual attack? Sometime our strength comes from the quite time, when we studing the Bible for ourselves. Spending an intimate moments with God. The main intent for worshiping is to study the Bible with clarity enough to get a simple understanding of what God want us to know about Him, His nature, His character and the life we're trying to live by "Faith" and believing in His Word – that His Son demonstrated. The "Perspicuity of the Scripture" does not mean that every passage we hear from our pastor we will understand it but how can we when we don't take the time to read the Bible for ourselves. Most of us don't have the highly education in theology, to comprehend the truth meaning that's coming from our pastor's because we are still in our sinful state of mind. And this is why we leave the church service not knowing what the pastor just preacher about!

According to the NIV Quiet Time Bible in 1 Corinthians 2:13-14 that says, "This is what we speak, not in words taught us by human wisdom but in words taught by the Spirit, expressing spiritual truths in spiritual words. The man without the Spirit does not accept the things that come from the Spirit of God, for they are foolishness to him, and he cannot understand them, because they are spiritually discerned." We have to be careful because distractions require our focus on something we should not be focusing on, and this is why we need the "Spirit of Discernment" to allow us to know the difference between a good spirit and a bad spirit. Not every spirit is from God and not everyone who prophesizes is from God, and this is why we should test every spirit that come our way. And all because we are testing spirits it doesn't mean that we are testing God. This may be hard to accept that some people are just evil, so before taking the other person word as face value; we must investigate to see if the information is true! Before we repeat something we just heard and the process violating the Second Greatest Commandment by lying and spreading rumors. And this how we find otherself worshiping the devil because he is the father of lies. We have to stop underestimate the power of the devil with his evil scheme that's going around attacking the truth, according to the NIV Quiet Time Bible in Romans 1:18-20 that says, "The wrath of God is being revealed from heaven against all the godlessness and wickedness of men who suppress the truth by their wickedness, since what may be known about God is plain to them, because God has make it plain to them.

For since the creation of the world God's invisible qualities – his eternal power and divine nature – have been clearly seen, being understood from what has been made, so that men are without excuse." Now, when some people do evil they do not consider the wrath of God! Why not? I don't know! Because there are different elements to the wrath of God, for example: There's Eternal hell or the lake of fire, eschatological wrath – which is defined by the prophets especially in the Book of Revelation. There is cataclysmic wrath – tsunamis, hurricanes, earthquakes, but the wrath that God has for those men who suppressing the truth on purpose: There will be a special wrath for them! Even the unbeliever is responsible for knowing the truth, therefore they are found guilty, because the word of God was made plain and with clarity to everyone. According to the Book of Romans 2:1-3 that says, "You, therefore, have no excuse, you who pass judgment on someone else, for at whatever point you judge the other, you are condemning yourself, because you who pass judgment do the same things. Now we know that God's judgment against those who do such things is based on truth. So, when you, a mere man, pass judgment on them and yet do the same things, do you think you will escape God's judgment?" And in Romans 1:21-23 that says, "For although they knew God, they neither glorified him as God nor gave thanks to him, but their thinking became futile, and their foolish hearts were darkened. Although they claimed to be wise, they became fools and exchanged the glory of the immortal God for images made to look like mortal man and birds and animals and reptiles."

This is the wrath that came down from heaven, according to the NIV Quiet Time Bible in Romans 1:24-32 that says, "Therefore, God gave them over in the sinful desires of their hearts to sexual impurity for the degrading of their bodies with one another: They exchanged the truth of God for a lie, and worshiped and served created things rather than the Creator – who is forever, praised (God) Amen. Because of this, God gave them over to shameful lusts. Even their women exchanged natural relations for unnatural ones. In the same way the men also abandoned natural relations with women and were inflamed with lust for one another. Men committed indecent acts with other men and received in themselves the due penalty for their perversion. Furthermore, since they did not think it worthwhile to retain the knowledge of God, he gave them over to a depraved mind to do what ought not to be done. They have become filled with every kind of wickedness, evil, greed and depravity. They are full of envy, murder, strife, deceit and malice. They are gossips, slanderers, God-haters, insolent, arrogant and boastful; they invent ways of doing evil, they disobey their parents; they are senseless, faithless, heartless, (and) ruthless. Although they know God's righteous decree that those who do such things deserve death, they not only continue to do these very things but also approve of those who practice them." With so many distractions going on in the world now is the time to decide whether or not to obey the word of God or to continue to walk in the order of disobedience. The purpose or the calling that God has placed on other people lives is for no one to take away or interfere with by playing the role of Judas.

Being envy and jealous of other people blessing is wrong! Everyone of us can testify about the goodness and the blessing that God, and how He at one point done something that was good in our life or defended us in some of your battles against the devil. And overcame one of your biggest problem that were trying to take our life so we all have a testimony of victory. Now, the question is? Why do you choice to destroy or interfere with someone else blessing and do the work of devil, when God has been so good in your life? Stop letting distractions be our downfall!

CHAPTER FOUR
Birth Pain

There's no other book other then the Bible that can tell the beginning of creation to the end of creation with a broad range of world events, authoritatively without revealing the time and date of the world as we know it! However, using biblical time to prepare us for the events that going to take place right here on earth. According to the NIV Quiet Time Bible in Acts 17:31 that says, "For he has set a day when he will judge the world with justice by the man he has appointed. He has given proof of this to all men by raising him from the dead." The Bible is full of predictions it contains about 735 about the future, and the Bible is a prophetic textbook, which approximately 596 predictions that has come true according to the Scriptures. This means; about 81% of the Bible prophecies came true, even though some of these were centuries ago but we have to believe that the remaining 19% or 139 prophecies will happen soon. And this will proof that the Bible is 100% accurate, the time period we are living in today is called: Birth Pain. In Romans 8:18-23 that says, "I consider that our present sufferings are not worth comparing with the glory that will be revealed in us. The creation waits in eager expectation for the sons of God to be revealed.

For the creation was subjected to frustration, not by its own choice, but by the will of the one who subjected it, in hope that the creation itself will be liberated from its bondage to decay and brought into the glorious freedom of the children of God. We know that the whole creation has been groaning as in the pains of childbirth right up to the present time. Not only so, but we ourselves, who have the first fruits of the Spirit, groan inwardly as we wait eagerly for our adoption as sons, the redemption of our bodies." It's the earth that groaning and waiting for the second coming of the Messiah, from the bondage of sin, death and decay, according to 2 Peter 3:12-13 that says, "As you look forward to the day of God and speed its coming: That day will bring about the destruction of the heavens by fire, and the elements will melt in the heat. But in keeping with his promise, we are looking forward to a New Heaven and a New Earth, the home of righteousness." Our Messiah told us to watch out that no one be deceives, according to Matthew 24:4-8 that says, "Jesus answered: Watch out that no one deceives you. For many will come in my name, claiming, I am the Christ, and will deceive many. You will hear of wars and rumors of wars but see to it that you are not alarmed. Such things must happen, but the end is still to come. Nation will rise against nation, and kingdom against kingdom. There will be famines and earthquakes in various places. All these are the beginning of birth pains." No one will know the day or the hour when these things will happen; now let's discuss the signs. There will be an increase of national disasters in the world however it will get blamed on climate change.

The real danger is deception by suppressing the truth and perception, which are the scheme of the devil that will take place inside and outside the church. The Bible already told us not to be alarmed and we shouldn't worry when we recognize some of these signs because they are just birth pains. Therefore as believers we might have to become a social misfit in the world because our citizenship is in the heavenly realm. Remember, as believer we are unique and our uniqueness stands out when we are not partaker of the world meaning: We cannot go with the flow or do what everybody else is doing! According to the NIV Quiet Time Bible in John 15:19 that says, "If you belonged to the world, it would love you as its own. As it is, you do not belong to the world, but I have chosen you out of the world. That is why the world hates you." It's not fun to be despised! We may witness the abomination of desolation that going to happen in the land of Israel, where our Messiah was crucified, and a man will appear to establish peace in that land the very city of God – Jerusalem: Will be known as the - Antichrist!

CHAPTER FIVE
Kata Tupos – According to the passages!

To learned who are the two nations, according to Genesis 25:21-26 that says, "Isaac prayed to the LORD on behalf of his wife, because she was barren. The LORD answered his prayer, and his wife Rebekah became pregnant. The babies jostled each other within her, and she said, why is this happening to me? So, she went to inquire of the LORD. The LORD said to her: Two nations are in your womb, and two people from within you will be separated; one people will be stronger than the other, and the older will serve the younger. When the time came for her to give birth, there were twin boys in her womb. The first to come out was red, and his whole body was like a hairy garment, so they named him Esau. After this, his brother came out, with his hand grasping Esau's heel; so, he was named Jacob. Isaac was sixty years old when Rebekah gave birth to them." And today it's these two nations that are still struggling with each other but what about kingdom against kingdom? And who are the kingdoms? Can it be the kingdom of light vs the kingdom of darkness?

According to Revelation 12:7-12 that says, "And there was war in heaven: Michael and his angels fought against the dragon, and the dragon and his angels fought back. But he was not strong enough, and they lost their place in heaven. The great dragon was hurled down – that ancient serpent called the devil, or Satan, who leads the whole world astray. He was hurled to the earth, and his angels with him. Then I heard a loud voice in heaven say: Now have come the salvation and the power and the kingdom of our God, and the authority of his Christ. For the accuser of our brothers, who accuses them before our God day and night, has been hurled down. They overcame him by the blood of the Lamb and by the word of their testimony; they did not love their lives so much as to shrink from death.   Therefore, rejoice you heavens and you who dwell in them! But woe to the earth and the sea because the devil has gone down to you! He is filled with fury because he knows that his time is short." And in Colossians 1:10-14 that says, "And we pray this in order that you may live a life worthy of the Lord and may please him in every way bearing fruit in every good work, growing in the knowledge of God, being strengthened with all power according to his glorious might so that you may have great endurance and patience, and joyfully giving thanks to the Father, who has qualified you to share in the inheritance of the saints in the kingdom of light. For he has rescued us from the dominion of darkness and brought us into the kingdom of the Son he loves, in whom we have redemption the forgiveness of sins."

Remember, it was said: All these are the beginning of the birth pains - nations will rise against nations, and kingdom against kingdom, there will be famines and earthquakes in various places, all of these things will happen together at once!

CHAPTER SIX

Kata Tupos – According to what has been written!

According to the NIV Quiet Time Bible in Matthew 24:37-44 that says, "As it was in the days of Noah, so it will be at the coming of the Son of Man: For in the days before the flood, people were eating and drinking, marrying and giving in marriage, up to the day Noah entered the ark; and they knew nothing about what would happen until the flood came and took them all away. That is how it will be at the coming of the Son of Man. Two men will be in the field, one will be taken and the other left. Two women will be grinding with a hand mill, one will be taken and the other left. Therefore, keep watch, because you do not know on what day your Lord will come. But understand this: If the owner of the house had known at what time of night the thief was coming, he would have kept watch and would not have let his house be broken into. So, you also must be ready, because the Son of Man will come at an hour when you do not expect him." On May 18, 1958 – Mike Wallace interviewed Aldous Huxley, author of the book "Brave New World" describing a future too close for comfort as political and economic freedom diminishes and sexual freedom increasing.

And he when on in talks about the dangers of world overpopulation, meaning people will have less food to eat and fewer goods to use per capita which seems to push towards a totalitarian regime without realizing it! We might be closer to the Book of Revelation Ch. 13, then we think; making way for the mark of the beast, which may occur when all government around the world establishes a cashless society. We already have facial recognition techniques and with the use of satellites – the government can monitor individuals in certain places on a global scale. So, the only way the Antichrist can bring forth his mark is by technology and artificial intelligence. China and Russia are leading the way with digital currency and social media will play a major role with a website-based application that enables users to create and share content or to participate in social networking. Social media has helped make the 21st century an open society, but it is an excellent marketing tool for promoting information that offers opportunities for employment and it's a non-stop learning tool. Therefore, we cannot believe everything we see or hear on social media, because it can play to our disadvantage and on our mental state of mind, meaning on our liberal democracy. Liberal democracy emphasizes separation of power and an independent judiciary system of checks and balances between branches of government.

Multi-party systems with at least two persistent viable political parties that are characteristics of liberal democracies and the rule of law in everyday life as part of an open society and market economy with private property, with equal protection of "Human Rights and Civil Rights, which bring Civil Liberties and Political Freedoms" for all people. However liberal democracies often draw upon the Constitution, to enshrine a social contract but after a period of expansion in the second half of the 20th century. Liberal democracy became a prevalent political system in the world but today in the 21st century: Mr. William Galston, stated our liberal democracy are in crisis with the rise of anti-pluralist populist movements caused by a combination of economic factors and migration; we need to take these concerns seriously, instead of feeling morally superior. In the U.S., this will require reintegration our economy so that small towns and rural areas thrive again; breaking through government gridlock; and purging the poison of our immigration policies. Mr. Galston is a Brookings senior fellow, a Wall Street Journal columnist, and academic, and former White House domestic policy advisor to President Bill Clinton. Now, why is this topic important? Because some people are afraid that the Constitution of the United States, may have to be rewritten, to fit all citizens of the United States of America and along with our National Anthem. It's this factor that's making people upset. However, on March 9, 2022, President Biden signed into law Executive Order 14067 aims at developing a digital assets policy plan and organizes federal regulators efforts in this area.

The order outlines five main goals, which include protection of consumers and investors, monetary stability, decreasing financial and national security risks, economic competitiveness, and responsible innovation. It also asks for more work to be done into developing a United States Central Bank Digital Currency (CBDC). But in section 4, it sets the stage for legal government surveillance of all U.S., citizens and total control over bank accounts and purchases. This means the government is coming after the paper dollar making it obsolete by replacing it with programmable digital tokens. The government will have the power to turn money on or off at will. China and Russia have already launched pilot programs for their own digital currencies almost 90% of central banks are testing or exploring digital currency, possibility by the end of 2024 or 2026, the standard of the U.S. dollar since 1792 will be replaced with a new currency – the digital dollar. Is it possible that this type of technology is preparing the way for the mark of the beast? It had been predicted that we would have no way of knowing what shape or form that the mark of the beast may appear, but what is important? Is our relationship with God through the His Son and the Holy Spirit – Honor your Mother! The Messiah: Is our salvation from the great tribulation. According to the NIV Quiet Time Bible in 1 Thessalonians 4:14-18 that says, "We believe that Jesus died and rose again and so we believe that God will bring with Jesus those who have fallen asleep in him: According to the Lord's own word, we tell you that we who are still alive, who are left till the coming of the Lord, will certainly not precede those who have fallen asleep.

For with a loud command, with the voice of the archangel and with the trumpet call of God, and the dead in Christ will rise first. After that, we who are still alive and are left will be caught up together with them in the clouds to meet the Lord in the air. And so, we will be with the Lord forever. Therefore encourage each other with these words."

CHAPTER SEVEN
Mentoring Importance

It's really important for everyone to have a mentor or a coach in their life like a navigation system, to give a real-time advice or help when it comes down to decisions making or giving a step-by-step direction of how to avoid heart breaking mistakes and help with getting to the final destination in life. A mentor or a coach can be compared to a navigation system because of their functions are basically the same, they are the experts with the experience that able to help or or give advice to the mentee helping with their career or with their talent to arrive at his/her destination on time. Everyone needs a little guidance or a little help to get where they want to go in life or career. This is the real reason mentoring is important! With the right mentor we can learn what to do, and what not to do, professionally and personally. Also they can become a big brother, a big sister, a mother or a father that you never had, and they can help accelerate a person's trajectory in life or career. Over-all the best thing about a mentor or a coach is "Availability" being there when things get hard or difficult. When deciding, or when circumstance in life get tough or when we just need that right person to talk to. We need mentorship like never before formal and informal especially the Millennials and Generation Z.

We have to teach them about financial decision making, when is the right time to get married, and when is the right time to start a family. Our black culture is fading right in front of our eyes and it's becoming a pandemic. Because of lack of mentorship, and we are falling behind professionally and financially. It's said that millennials are projected to comprise more than 75% of the workforce by 2025, and with 79% of them saying mentoring is important to them so it's crucial that parents should start supporting their children dreams and helping them with their education in the area of skill development, time management and emotional intelligence: This can be a solution to the pandemic. That's effecting the black community with financial literacy and having a mentor on your job; 71% are more likely to stay employed at the same company that offer an opportunities for advancement. And 89% say their contributions are valued and 91% will say that they are satisfied being employed by their company and overall this is because of mentorship helps mentees learn faster and feel valuable. But there is a down side of being a mentee because they don't get the opportunity to pick their mentor. Because of diversity at the bottom doesn't necessarily make it to the top, the person have to be organic and sustainable to make it at the top or in other words meet the needs of the present without compromising who you are. Sometimes, what an organization needs is a different perspective on wisdom and knowledge, diversity can bring this in certain area of organization management. Sometime people need a little help in jump starting their career or help with life decisions.

However, a true mentor knows that mentorship is a two-way street and one of the hardest things to do as a mentor is to give constructive criticism. It's a valuable tool that allows the mentee to learn and grow and without constructive criticism – the mentee may keep on making the same mistakes. Fostering a strong sense that the organization values employee's development is crucial for the long-term success of any organization. And some of the reasons that employees quit their job is low pay, no opportunities for advancement and feeling disrespected. Most of the time, the mentor understands the mentee's struggles because they went through the same struggles themselves, and this puts a mentor in a unique position because they share the same core values as the mentee, so sometime they see themselves in them. Life is all about being proactive and productive – this is where a life coach comes into a person's life, he/she helps that person to take corrective action towards their lifegoals. They do this by asking questions, listening and raising self-awareness to uncover their true potential but the difference between a life coach and a mentor he/she doesn't have to share the same career path, but they do need to know, what's their specific goal or goals. Remember, life coaching isn't therapy, it's about helping the person move forward in life with a purpose and a strategy to be successful after high school however the parent plays the most important role mentoring, for example: College vs. Apprenticeship program, Military vs. Police or Fireman Academy.

And how to taking on financial responsibility, when to buy a home vs. apartment, when to open your first bank account or saving account, and the most important lesson; how to avoid costly mistakes and if you do make a mistake, how to prioritize your decisions because mistakes is a part of life. And a life coach will help with finding a creative solutions without judging they come in all shapes and forms to help people with their confidence especially in life/work balance, self-awareness, and help with implement changes when distractions occur. However, how do we know when we have the right person as a mentor or life coach? Whether you're starting a new career or jump starting your life to the next level, a good mentor or life coach can help navigate the process but they have to exhibit good character themselves. That will make them stand out from other people and capable and willing to invested their time to boost someone career or help them to reach their goals in life. These are just some of the characteristics to look for in a mentor or life coach: Do they values respect, you can easily tell if a person values respect just by the ways they interact with other people. Because they're professional, friendly and are respected by those around them, they will give honest and constructive feedback, they are problem-solver, active listeners and have no problem advocates on your behalf. They know the industry and willingly expanded your network, they motivate others to pursue their goals and they are always learning and willing to share their knowledge on what's trending. And the best thing about having a mentor or a life coach is that you can have more than one.

144

Once we acknowledge the mentor that's already in our body which is – the Holy Spirit. The mystery that will transform our life through pure spiritual knowledge of God grace that He has for our life when we walk in humility. According to the NIV Quiet Time Bible in James 4:6 that says, "But he gives us more grace. That is what Scripture says: God opposes the proud but give grace to the humble." Whatever God gives us, He can give us more of it, when we walk in humility, because everything that God give us it's a seed and can be multiplied; if it's wisdom He can give more, if it's leadership He can give more, and He has the power to give longevity just by being humble." And in Philippians 2:1-3 that says, "If you have an encouragement from being united with Christ, if any comfort from his love, if any fellowship with the Spirit, if any tenderness and compassion, then make my joy complete by being like-minded, having the same love, being one in spirit and purpose. Do nothing out of selfish ambition or vain conceit, but in humility consider others better than yourselves. Each of you should look not only to your own interests, but also to the interests of others." Also in 1 Peter 5:5-6 that says, "Young men(*women*), in the same way submissive to those who are older. All of you, clothe yourselves with humility toward one another, because, God opposes the proud but gives grace to the humble. Humble yourselves, therefore, under God's mighty hand, that he may lift you up in due time." What is the deceitfulness of pride and why do God despise prideful people? Because pride is deceitfulness and walk in its own deception believing things that are untrue.

145

Prideful people believe in their own accomplishments and have a negative attitude towards other people because pride is connected to boastfulness and perception, so every time pride shows up it is dragging destruction. According to Proverbs 16:18 that says "Pride goes before destruction, a haughty spirit before a fall." And in Proverbs 29:23 that says, "A man's pride brings him low, but a man of lowly spirit gains honor." In mentorship expectations have to be realistic because mentors are shortcuts to success and sometime in mentorship, they have to be willing to learn through the other person's pain and mistakes but don't forget to establish an clear boundaries.

CHAPTER EIGHT
The Hidden Truth – Apocrypha

In America, most churches read from the sixty-six books of the King James Version Bible (KJV), even though some may use the Ryrie Study Bible, with red letters highlighting the God's words however, there are many versions of the Bible. Matter of fact; there's over 5,000 New Testament manuscripts in Greek, and about 10,000 Old Testament manuscripts in Hebrew, also approximately 19,000 copies of manuscripts in Coptic, Latin Aramaic and in Syriac. When the King James Bible was first translated in 1611, only the Greek manuscripts were accessible than in 1881, a revised versions utilized the newest evidence to update the Bible. But by the twentieth century more than one hundred ancient Greek manuscripts have been discovered and they were written on papyrus (material prepared in ancient Egypt for writing or painting purpose). The Bible translations made before 1947 did not use the Dead Sea Scrolls Manuscripts, so the Bible had to be translated again to take advantage of these discoveries. The term "Apocrypha" comes from the Greek word meaning – hidden or secret, some people think these books are too exalted to be made available to the general public, but why?

The Apocrypha includes 15 or more books and one is found in the Septuagint, part 1 and 2 part of Esdras, which influenced by the Jewish cannon of the Old Testament. These books are: The First and Second Book of Esdras, The First and Second Book of Maccabees, The Book of Baruch, The Book of Bel and The Dragon, Ecclesiastes or The Preacher, The Book of Esther, The Book of Judith, The Prayer of Manasseh, The Song of Solomon, The History of Susanna, The Book of Tobit, and The Book of Wisdom. These books and more were excluded from the 1885 reprint of the King James Version of the Bible by American publishers. Because of anti-Catholic bias, some may say these books are not held equal to the Sacred Scriptures but yet, still the breath of God, and useful for studying. Reading these books will help enhance your understanding of the divinely inspired Scriptures, of the hidden secret of the Apocrypha, which first appeared in the Greek translation of the Old Testament called the Septuagint. Which was produced around 200 BC., the individual books that constitute the Apocrypha were written roughly between 400 BC and AD 1, this period of time is frequently referred to as "The Four Hundred Silent Years." Therefore, as we know one day in heaven is like a thousand years on earth: This essentially makes up for that blank page in our Bible between Malachi and Matthew: So, was this period of time were actually 4,000 years? In a pejorative sense these writings contain mysterious, sometimes profound mysterious and hard to comprehend; they are called hidden secrets for a good reason.

Some of these books are known as "Deuterocanonical" rather than the Apocrypha like: Maccabees 3 & 4, The Prayer of Azariah, The Prayer of Manasseh, Psalm 51 and The Letter of Jeremiah. And the Apocrypha is proof; how old the earth really is through Biblical history, not science. According to the NIV Quiet Time Bible in Jeremiah 36:26 that says, "Instead, the king commanded Jerahmeel, a son of the king, Seraiah son of Azriel and Shelemiah son of Abdeel to arrest Baruch the scribe and Jeremiah, the prophet: But the LORD had hidden them. In the Old Testament it was told that King Manasseh - he was a wicked king over the Southern Kingdom of Israel, however he repented after being imprisoned by the King of Assyria. Then and only then he humbled himself and God restored his kingdom, according to the NIV Quiet Time Bible in 2 Chronicles 33:10-13 that says, "The LORD spoke to Manasseh and his people, but they paid no attention. So, the LORD brought against them the army commanders of the King of Assyria, who took Manasseh prisoner, put a hook in his nose, bound him with bronze shackles and took him to Babylon. In his distress he sought the favor of the LORD his God and humbled himself greatly before the God of his fathers. And when he prayed to him, the LORD was moved by his entreaty and listened to his plea; so, he brought him back to Jerusalem, and to his kingdom. Then Manasseh knew that the LORD is God." The prayer of King Manasseh moved God so much during the silent years that He acted on his behalf, and this prayer can be found in the Book of the lost Chronicles of the Kings of Israel.

At the age of five God introduced Daniel in the Story of Susanna, the Holy Spirit came on him to save Suanna life and exposed Daniel again in Bel and the Dragon but the most important find we can discover is our Spiritual Mother – the Holy Spirit, in the book of Wisdom of Solomon. Methuselah was Adam's oldest righteous grandson that lived to an age of 969, died seven days before the "Great Flood" and he was a Great Hebrew Patriarch, in the blood line of Kings. But after the Great Flood, God reduced life to 120 years and today not too many people reach or live past 120 years because of wickedness and sin of mankind. So it took our Spiritual Mother through a woman to make the second blood sacrifice by man, to restore mankind relationship back with God. Every Black person would do well knowing the truth about where the Black race stands in Biblical history because it's all about the truth of who we are! When the Messiah entered into Jerusalem riding a donkey, and the people spread palm branches on the ground, that was a spiritual symbol of power and victory over the oppressors during the Maccabean revolt, according to the NIV Quiet Time Bible in John 12:12-15 that says, "The next day the great crowd that had come for the Feast heard that Jesus was on his way to Jerusalem. They took palm branches and went out to meet him, shouting, Hosanna! Blessed is he who comes in the name of the Lord! Blessed is the King of Israel! Jesus found a young donkey and sat upon it, as it is written: Do not be afraid, O Daughter of Zion; see, your king is coming, seated on a donkey's colt." And in 2 Kings, the Jews were, in fact, celebrating in anticipation of a bloody coup.

Jehu's violent actions are a far cry from our vision of a Palm Sunday celebration, but these were the types of actions the Jews were anticipating as they placed their cloaks and branches in Jesus' path. The most historic story that acknowledge Jesus as our king; was during Jesus – triumphal entry. In 168 BC, the Seleucid king, Antiochus Epiphanes, put down one Jewish revolt, reconquered Jerusalem after a second revolt and executed many Jewish leader, please read 2 Maccabees 5:11-14. To add injury to insult, Antiochus erected a statue of Zeus inside the Jewish Temple and sacrificed a pig on their altar of incense this act was the abomination of desolation that's in Daniel 9:27. It was the light that came out of the era of spiritual darkness, foretold by the Apostle Paul, in his second letter to Thessalonians, about the "Great Apostasy" which resulted in the establishment of the Papal Power. Satan once endeavored to form a compromise with the Messiah, by coming to him in the wilderness. And Satan showed the Messiah, all the kingdoms in the world and the glory of them; then Satan offered to give all into the Messiah hands, if He would acknowledge Satan as the supremacy prince of darkness, however, the Messiah rebuked him forcing Satan to depart. Today, the leading Doctrine of Romanism is the Pope: Whoever sits in that seat is the visible head of the Universal Church of Christ, invested with supreme authority over the bishops and pastors in all parts of the world.

The Pope has been given the titles of deity and he has been styled "Lord God the Pope" and has declared infallible demanding homage of all men, and the same claim urged by Satan in the wilderness of temptation is still urged by him through the Church of Rome. According to Isaiah 53, is proof that our Messiah is a Black man! This alone is a very bold statement because God is – Almighty, and He cannot lie, for all of God's works are just, true and righteous. The Apocrypha books are theologically illumination and spiritually uplifting that's un-orthodox writing in should be read for devotional. They are divine Scriptures for whoever wants to grow on a different spiritual level, and it can fill in some historical gaps that are missing from the Bible. These books can prove that our ancestors are the original Black Jewish Nation of Israel - that once lived in the land called: Israel. Also the Apocrypha will help identify the fall of kings and give witness of how the Pharisees became so politically powerful. And how the Romans Empire became the rule over Israel, but most importantly, it will give the reader a good understanding of Black Biblical history. According to the NIV Quiet Time Bible in Habakkuk 1:13 that says, "Your eyes are too pure to look on evil; you cannot tolerate wrong. Why then do you tolerate the treacherous? Why are you silent while the wicked swallow up those more righteous than themselves?" Another book to read is called: The Gospel of Thomas, which was discovered near Nag Hammadi, Egypt in December of 1945: Among a group of books known as the Nag Hammadi library.

These are just some of the secret sayings which the living Messiah spoke and which Didymos Judas Thomas wrote down. And this book will teach us about fasting and informed Black people about the origin of our skin color, according to the Gospel of Thomas 50:1-3 that says, "If they ask you; where do you come from? (then) say to them, we have come from the light, the place where the light has come into being by itself, has established (itself) and has appeared in their image. If they ask you; what is the sign of your God among you? Then say to them: It is movement and repose." Or in other words – the Bible's plots movements of creation, the fall of mankind, redemption and the coming of the kingdom are explored to understand the Bible's message. Also the Bible stories explained how God plans is unveiled through His covenants in Christ. Also repose means: Sabbath or Rest. The Messiah is quoted in Gospel of Thomas 77 that say, "It is I who Am the light which is above them all. It is I who Am the all from me did all come forth and unto me did the all extend. Split a piece of wood and I Am there, lift up a stone and you will find me there, the consciousness lives in everything, and everyone is curious when will the Kingdom of Heavens is going to come. It will not come by waiting for it, and it will not be a matter of saying, here it is, or there it is, rather the Kingdom of the Father is spread out upon the earth and men do not see it."

In other words, the Kingdom of Heaven, is connected to everything and everyone, it is a gift based on the power of the Holy Spirit, to manifest by using the power of thoughts and our emotional intelligence, that we already have within us, according to the Gospel of Thomas's 114 sayings of Jesus verse 3 that says, "If those who lead you say to you, see, the kingdom is in the sky; then the birds of the sky will precede you. If they say to you, it is in the sea; then the fish will precede you. Rather, the kingdom is inside of you, and it is outside of you. When you come to know yourselves; then you will become known, and you will realize that it is you who are the sons of the living father. But if you will not know yourselves, you dwell in poverty, and it is you who are that poverty." With our creative thoughts we have the power within us to manifest things into reality. According to the NIV Quiet Time Bible in John 16:23-24 that says, "In that day you will no longer ask me anything. I tell you the truth, my Father will give you whatever you ask in my name. Until now you have not asked for anything in my name. Ask and you will receive, and your joy will be complete." Therefore, we have the power to change our circumstances by just speaking and believing in the power that is in us - the Holy Spirit. Using the words of God when we pray to the Father, He is looking at our heart desires but only if it's in alignment to His will. And we are instructed to be a blessing to others however we cannot have any resentment, animosity, or hate in our heart toward anyone, because it's our heart that speak to the living God our heavenly Father.

According to the Gospel of Thomas 101 that says, "Whoever does not love his father and his mother in my way, shall not be able to become a disciple to me. For my mother bore my body yet, my true Mother gave me after - life." And the Book of Jubilees is important to read because it explains the present and future events also the division of days, weeks and years using the "Hebrew Calendar" which played a significant role in preserving social cohesion to the Nation of the Israelites. This was revealed to Moses, along with the Torah instruction, on top of Mount Sinai by the Angel of the Lord – which is Christ: And this is why he told the Pharisees that He spoke with Moses. It was Moses who received the instruction about how to use the lunar calculations to track the Jubilees Celebration of Festivals that was practiced by our earlier ancestors, Noah, Abraham and other patriarchs before renewing of the covenant that was to come. Among the nine hundred or so texts of the "Dead Sea Scrolls" it's the Book of Jubilees, retelling Genesis and Exodus in the original writing in Hebrew. Approximately fifty chapters that report the events in chronological order of a 49-year period from the creation until Moses received the commandments on Mount Sinai. We understand that the "Great Gathering" is going to happen first, but the second coming of the Messiah is going to happen during the next Jubilees year so when is the next Jubilees year? But can we find the answer to this question in the Bible?

155

According to the NIV Quiet Time Bible in Leviticus 25:1-5 that says, "The LORD said to Moses on Mount Sinai, speak to the Israelites and say to them: When you enter the land, I am going to give you, the land itself must observe a Sabbath to the LORD. For six years sow your fields, and for six years prune your vineyards and gather their crops. But in the seventh year the land is to have a Sabbath of rest, a Sabbath to the LORD. Do not sow your fields or prune your vineyards. Do not reap what grows of itself or harvest the grapes of your untended vines. The land is to have a year of rest." Mankind cannot predict the Jubilees based on what we think because no man know the day or hour for our Messiah to return. Therefore, every ten years is a decade but dealing with the Jubilees, God told the Israelites to divide their time in seven year increments meaning "Shibui" because of six days and one day of rest equal seven and that seventh day is known as the – Sabbath. The Israelites supposed to let the land rest in the seven year and they also supposed to rest and this is the concept of the "Sabbatical Years" and they supposed to count off seven years periods to the 49 years. According to Leviticus 25:8-9 that says, "Count off seven Sabbaths of years – seven times seven years – so that the seven Sabbaths of years amount to a period of forty nine years. Then have the trumpet sounded everywhere on the tenth day of the seventh month; on the Day of Atonement sound the trumpet throughout your land." This is what the Israelites called a Jubilee cycle which is the year after or the fiftieth year – making it the Jubilee.

According to the NIV Quiet Time Bible in Leviticus 25:10-11 that says, "Consecrate the fiftieth year and proclaim liberty throughout the land to all its inhabitants: It shall be a jubilee for you, each one of you is to return to his family property and each to his own clan. The fiftieth year shall be a jubilee for you; do not sow and do not reap what grows of itself or harvest the untended vines." And in the end time this will be fulfilled by all "True Israelites" returning to their land, but this has not happened yet! What so special about the Book of Jubilees, it tells us all the major Jubilees cycle and events that happen since the beginning of creation and it dated back years before the Messiah, using the forty nine years of the Jubilees cycles. According to the NIV Quiet Time Bible in 2 Timothy 3:16-17 that says, "All Scripture is God-breathed and is useful for teaching, rebuking, correcting and training in righteousness, so that the man of God may be thoroughly equipped for every good work." Now we can talk about the 70 Weeks Prophecy of Daniel – according to Daniel 9:24 that says, "Seventy sevens (weeks) are decreed for your people and your holy city to finish transgression to put an end to sin, to atone for wickedness, to bring in everlasting righteousness, to seal up vision and prophecy and to anoint the most holy." If we put these weeks into Jubilee cycles of 49 years, we come up with exactly ten Jubilees cycles and Daniel, understood this with the help from an angle, and he divide the prophecy into three periods of 7 weeks and a periods of 62 weeks and a final period of one week; which equal the 70th week of Daniel or we can called this the "Tribulation Period."

157

And we can follow up by reading a book called: 70 Times 7 Daniel's Mysterious Countdown and the Church's Heroic Future, by: Nelson Walters. But the last in final week of Daniel's Prophecy has not happened yet, which means the final week of the Jubilee has not happened yet! Biblically speaking we were told that after the 62 weeks the Messiah, was to be cut off or his crucifixion, according to Daniel 9:26 that says, "After the sixty-two sevens the Anointed One will be cut off and will have nothing. The people of the ruler who will come will destroy the city and the sanctuary. The end will come like a flood: War will continue until the end, and desolations have been decreed." So can we say, that we're not too far off from the final week of the Jubilees cycle, which maybe between the years of 2049 – 2050 or sooner; meaning the Great Gathering might happen or are we are just waiting on the Messiah second coming? Remember, that no one knows the day or the hour of his second coming. In Daniel 9:24, when the Angel Gabriel appears to Daniel, he promises him ten jubilee cycles and nine of them already happen meaning; we are just waiting on the final week cycle of Daniel's 70th Weeks Prophecy. Please, understand that no one is trying to set a date for the Messiah second coming or the Great Gathering, but we were told to be watchful and to look for the signs, so this is not crying wolf. There is another mystery that's in the Bible that being overlook because some people reply that the word "Rapture" is not in the Bible. However, let's investigate in the NIV Quiet Time Bible in Revelation 12:5 that says, "She gave birth to a son, a male child, who will rule all the nations with an iron scepter. And her child was snatched up to God and to his throne."

The Greek term "Harpazo" has the same meaning for "Snatched up" and in the New Testament, the word "Harpazo" is used for the word "Rapture," caught up, or caught away however five times out of thirteen, it appears in the Bible relating to the rapture. The other eight times it is translated, to forcibly seize upon, snatch away, take to oneself or use force on someone so this means the word "Rapture" do appear in the Bible, and the Messiah did ascend to heaven in a form of a rapture. According to the NIV Quiet Time Bible in Hosea 6:2 that says, "After two days he will revive us: On the third day he will restore us that we may live in his presence." We all know that our Messiah rose from the dead on the third day after his crucifixion but in the Bible we were told a thousand years is like a day in heaven. According to Psalm 90:4 that says, "For a thousand years in your sight are like a day that has just gone by or like a watch in the night." And in Luke 12:38 that says, "It will be good for those servants whose master finds them ready, even if he comes in the second or third watch of the night." 2 Peter 3:8 that says, "But do not forget this one thing, dear friends: With the Lord a day is like a thousand years, and a thousand years are like a day." Now, can we dare say, literally, it took God, six thousand years for God to finish his creation and the last thousand years which equal one day that he set it apart for himself as a – Sabbath? Now! Due this mean six thousand years has pass and we are waiting on the "Rapture" to spend one thousand years of rest with the Messiah?

Also in 2 Peter 3:3-7 that say, "First of all, you must understand that in the last days scoffers will come, scoffing and following their own evil desires. They will say, where is this coming, he promised? Ever since our fathers died, everything goes on as it has since the beginning of creation. But they deliberately forget that long ago by God's word the heavens existed and the earth was formed out of water and by water. *(And who is the living water).* By these waters also the world of that time was deluged and destroyed. By the same word, the present heavens and earth are reserved for fire, being kept for the Day of Judgment and Destruction of ungodly men." But what we don't know is that everything is related to the seven days creation narrative and that each day is equal to one thousand years. So six days is literally six thousand years biblically speaking because it has been 4,000 years from the creation and after the Messiah death it been 2,000 years that the Messiah ascends to heaven. Therefore, remember that no one knows the day or the hour for the day of the Lord. However, in the NIV Quiet Time Bible in Revelation 2:14-17 that says, "Nevertheless, I have a few things against you: You have people there who hold to the teaching of Balaam, who taught Balak to entice the Israelites to sin by eating food sacrificed to idols and by committing sexual immorality. Likewise, you also have those who hold to the teaching of the Nicolaitans. Repent therefore!

Otherwise, I will soon come to you and will fight against them with the sword of my mouth. He who has an ear, let him hear what the Spirit says to the churches. To him who overcomes, I will also give him a white stone with a new name written on it, known only to him who receives it." And in 1 John 5:21 that says, "Dear children, keep yourselves from idols." But who and what are the Nicolaitans? And why does God hate them so much? They practiced the teaching of adultery, like many did in ancient times and they served the pagan god who practiced child sacrifice. According to Leviticus 20:2-5 that says, "The LORD said to Moses: Say to the Israelites, any Israelite or any alien living in Israel who gives any of his children to Molech must be put to death. The people of the community are to stone him. I will set my face against that man, and I will cut him off from his people; for by giving his children to Molech, he had defiled my sanctuary and profaned my holy name. If the people of the community close their eyes when that man gives on of his children to Molech and they fail to put him to death, I will set my face against that man and his family and will cut off from their people both him and all who follow him in prostituting themselves to Molech. There's one church that stands out from all the other pagan churches because of the child sacrifices and the Apostle John wrote remarks against the "Temple of Diana or the Greek goddess – Artemis, but how did this pagan goddess find her way into today's churches? By "Idolatry" - extreme admiration for the love of money or reverence for something or someone for example like people worshiping or worshiping the man or woman that giving the message.

161

The first of the biblical Ten Commandments prohibits idolatry – You shall have no other gods before me! This is considered wickedness, worshiping other gods is what drove King Solomon insane. And now believers are adding secular music and holiday traditions to blend in with Scripture: According to the NIV Quiet Time Bible in Ezekiel 8:18 that says, "Therefore I will deal with them in anger: I will not look on them with pity or spare them. Although they shout in my ears, I will not listen to them." Paganism was the thing that Abraham was called out of - and Moses put a stop to it. Elijah stood up against it and this was called the Great Confrontation on Mount Carmel. Today, churches are brought up under tradition so it's hard to break bad habits even to accept the "Kingdom Message of the Messiah" because the pastors are still telling stories about Christmas and Easter. Mentally we are taken captive by worshiping false scripture and tradition therefore man cannot break the "Second Blood Covenant" throughout our history in America, it has been a struggle identifying ourselves in Black Biblical History about who we are! So: Please watch the documentary called: Who We Are – A Chronicle of Racism in America. It's a powerful lecture and archive of information from a civil rights lawyer named – Jeffery Robinson. His point of view draws a sobering timeline of anti-Black racism in the United States.

According to Isaiah 41:8-10 that says, "But you, O Israel my servant Jacob, whom I have chosen, you descendants of Abraham my friend, I took you from the ends of the earth, from its farthest corners I called you. I said, you are my servant: I have chosen you and have not rejected you. So do not fear, for I am with you; do not be dismayed, for I am your God. I will strengthen you and help you, I will uphold you with my righteous right hand." Nevertheless, why are so many people curious about the author of the Book of Enoch? The confirmation is in the Book of Hebrews because we must have faith! According to the Book of Enoch 1:1-8 that says, "The words of the blessing of Enoch, wherewith he blessed the elect and righteous, who will be living in the day of tribulation, when all the wicked and godless are to be removed: And he took up his parable and said, Enoch a righteous man whose eyes were opened by God, saw the vision of the Holy One in the heavens which the angels showed me and from then I heard everything and from them I understood as I saw but not for this generation but for a remote one which is for to come. Concerning the elect, I said and took up my parable concerning them: The Holy Great One will come forth from his dwelling and the eternal God will tread upon the earth (even on Mount Sinai) and appear from his camp and appear in the strength of his might from the heaven of heavens. And all shall be smitten with fear and the watchers shall quake and great fear and trembling shall seize them unto the ends of the earth.

And the high mountains shall be shaken, and the high hills shall be made low and shall melt like wax before the flame. And the earth shall be wholly rent is sunder and all that is upon the earth shall perish and there shall be a judgement upon all (mankind). But with the righteous He will make peace. And will protect the elect and mercy shall be upon them and they shall all belong to God, and they shall be prospered, and they shall all be blessed. And He will help them all and light shall appear unto them, and He will make peace with them." These are the words from Enoch and how he blessed us, the elect and the righteous and it was God the Father, who opened Enoch eyes to see this holy vision that's going to take place in our generation. Please watch this YouTube channel called: The CIA Classified Book – about the Pole Shift, Mass Extinctions and The True Adam & Eve Story. The CIA only released fifty-seven pages of the original 284-page manuscript and those pages have been, in the CIA's own words – sanitized. This is just an ideal about how's it going to look when the end times happen.

CHAPTER NINE
As Above So Below

The Book of Enoch is full of hidden secrets, and it should be honored as Scripture because both Enoch and Moses received the same testimony from the heavenly tablets. Which are in heaven and was given to the children of God. Enoch was the only prophet that got a grand tour of all the heavens, and went down to the center of the earth or the hollow earth. And was taught the Torah and cosmology by angels also to be daring; it was Enoch that was the first man on the moon – a Black man. The overview of the Books of Enoch – which was removed from the Bible, this book among other things, describes an ancient time with an ancient calendar. Which unsurprisingly has come to be known as the Enoch Calendar. This ancient Enoch Calendar: While it may seem similar on the surface, differs from our modern Gregorian calendar in a significant and affecting way. The Books of Enoch contain astronomical knowledge as it was given to Enoch by the Archangel Uriel, during Enoch's trips through the heavens. And addition to the calendar itself, the Archangel Uriel bestows upon Enoch information relation to Laws of God, by which the sun, moon, stars, and winds are governed as well as other mysteries of the Universe.

These are three books in one the first: Enoch 1 – An ancient Jewish text attributed to Enoch, containing the visions, the prophecies, and the celestial hierarchy influential in Jewish and apocalyptic literature. Enoch 2 – A lesser-known text in Slavic languages, explores Enoch's heavenly journeys and the visions part of the Slavonic Enoch tradition. Enoch 3 – Focuses on Enoch's transformation into the angel Metatron; part of the Jewish mystical traditions, and discusses cosmological and mystical themes. The understanding of cosmology is more than science, it's mind-blowing and this is where metaphysics come into play because the universe is like trying to understand what God was thinking, and this is proof that there is a God. Everything about God is true! However, there's one subject in today's churches that's not getting enough attention; which is the Book of Revelation! According to the NIV Quiet Time Bible in Revelation 3:1-3 that says, "These are the words of him who holds the Seven Spirits of God and the Seven Stars, I know your deeds; you have a reputation of being alive, but you are dead: Wake up! Strengthen what remains and is about to die, for I have not found your deeds complete in the sight of my God. Remember, therefore, what you have received and heard; obey it, and repent *(repent means: Change your mind!)*. But if you do not wake up, I will come like a thief, and you will not know at what time I will come to you." Sardis is one of the seven churches of Asia – remember the letter to seven churches represents "People."

According to Revelation 1:11 the Messiah said to
John, "Write on a scroll what you see and send it to the
Seven Churches: Ephesus, Smyrna, Pergamum, Thyatira,
Sardis, Philadelphia, and Laodicea." The Messiah gave John,
a specific message for each church – Sardis, West Central
Asia Minor, was the capital of the ancient Kingdom of Lydia,
a wealthy and important commercial trading center but it was
a pagan city that was home to the well-known Temple of
Artemis, which still exists today in ruins. The church at
Sardis was surrounded by paganism and idolatry, but failed
to stand out amidst the darkness, although they appeared to
be spiritual alive on the outside, but God knew their hearts
and He rebuked them. Is it possible for a church to have the
appearance of life while in reality, it's spiritually dead! Do
the modern-day churches need to take a careful spiritual
inventory of themselves and strengthen the things which
remain before they die? Of course! Therefore, the two
groups of sevens are explained according to Revelation 1:20
that says, "The mystery of the Seven Stars that you saw in
my right hand and of the Seven Golden Lampstands is this;
the Seven Stars are the Angels of the Seven Churches *(each
Angel representing a church on earth)* and the Seven Golden
Lampstands are the Seven churches." Now, this is just one
man opinion on the seven major religions on earth: Judaism,
Christianity, Islam, Hinduism, Sikhism, Buddhism and
Animism. But we know there's other religions!

According to the NIV Quiet Time Bible in Revelation 5:1-14 that says, "Then I saw in the right hand of him who sat on the throne a scroll with writing on both sides and sealed with seven seals. And I saw a mighty angel proclaiming in a loud voice, who is worthy to break the seals and open the scroll? But no one in heaven or on earth or under the earth could open the scroll or even look inside it. I wept and wept because no one was found who was worthy to open the scroll or look inside. Then one of the elders said to me, do not weep! See, the Lion of the Tribe of Judah, the Root of David, has triumphed. He is able to open the scroll and its seven seals. Then I saw a Lamb, looking as if it had been slain, standing in the center of the throne, encircled by the Four Living Creatures and the Elders. He had seven horns and seven eyes, which are the seven spirits of God sent out into all the earth. He took the scroll from the right hand of him who sat on the Throne. And when he had taken it, the Four Living Creatures and the Twenty-Four Elders fell down before the Lamb. Each one had a harp, and they were holding golden bowls full of incense, which are the prayers of the saints. And they sang a new song: You are worthy to take the scroll and open its seals, because you were slain, and with your blood you purchased men of God from every tribe, language, people, and nation. You have made them to be a Kingdom and Priest to serve our God, and they will reign on the earth. Then I looked and heard the voice of many angels, numbering thousands upon thousands, and ten thousand times ten thousand.

They encircled the throne and the Living Creatures and the Elders. In a loud voice they sang: Worthy is the Lamb, who was slain, to receive power, wealth, wisdom, strength, honor, glory, and praise! Then I heard every creature in heaven and on earth and under the earth and on the sea, and all that is in them, singing: To him who sits on the Throne and to the Lamb, be praise and honor, glory, and power, forever and ever! The Four Living Creatures said, Amen, and the Elders fell down and worshiped." The Secrets of Creation is in 2 Enoch (Slavonic) in 41:1-9 Enoch talks about his experience: The notion of "Secrets" occupies a distinct place in 2 Enoch. The importance of this terminology is highlighted by its prominent position in the title of the book. While various manuscripts of 2 Enoch are known under different titles, most of them include the word "Secrets" in some of these titles the term is connected with Enoch's books. The Secret Books of Enoch, the titles "Secrets" are linked to God – The Book's is called: The Secrets of God. A revelation to Enoch – himself! This consistency in the use of the term "Secrets," in spite of its varied attribution to different subjects, may indicate that the authors and/or the transmitters of the text viewed the motif "Secrets" as a central theme of the apocalypse. The purpose of this chapter is to call attention to some details of the theme "Secrets" in 2 Enoch. Moreover, it seems that in 2 Enoch the realm of secrets, even topologically, transcends the angelic world of metaphysics.

The shorter recension tells that before the cosmogonic revelation took place, the Lord had placed Enoch to the Left of Himself, closer than Gabriel. Further, God confirms the transcendence of the knowledge about creation over the angelic world, when He informed to Enoch and not to his angels explained neither secrets nor His endless and inconceivable creation which He conceived. The "Secrecy" of the God's revelation is underscored further by several additional factors: First, immediately following the cosmogonic instruction, He informed Enoch about the appointed time and the intercessor. God also informed Enoch about the Archangel Michael, and the Guardian Angels, Arioch and Marioch. And told Enoch that his writings will not perish in the impending flood. For I will give you an intercessor, Enoch, on the account of your handwriting and the handwriting of your fathers – Adam and Seth. They will not be destroyed until the final age, for I have commanded my angels Arioch and Marioch, whom I have appointed on the earth to guard them and to command the things of time to preserve the handwritings of your fathers so that they might not perish in the impending flood, which I will create in your generation (read 33:10-12). Please, please read the Books of Enoch, to get an understanding of who help Enoch write and author his books. And learned about the indescribable vision of the things he saw while touring the heavens because Enoch saw the immovable throne of God. And read the Book of Jasher – which means the Book of the Upright or the Book of the Just Man.

According to the NIV Quiet Time Bible in Isaiah 44:6-28 that says, "This is what the LORD says - Israel's King and Redeemer, the LORD Almighty: I am the first and I am the last; apart from me there is no God. Who then is like me? Let him proclaim it. Let him declare and lay out before me what has happened since I established my ancient people, and what is yet to come – yes, let him foretell what will come. Do not tremble, do not be afraid. Did I not proclaim this and foretell it long ago? You are my witnesses. Is there any God besides me? No, there is no other Rock; I know not one. All who make idols are nothing, and the things they treasure are worthless. Those who would speak up for them are blind; they are ignorant, to their own shame. Who shapes a god and casts an idol, which can profit him nothing? He and his kind will be put to shame; craftsmen are nothing but men. Let them all come together and take their stand; they will be brought down to terror and infamy. The blacksmith takes a tool and works with it in the coals; he shapes an idol with hammers, he forges it with the might of his arm. He gets hungry and loses his strength; he drinks no water and grows faint. The carpenter measures with a line and makes an outline with a marker; he roughs it out with chisels and marks it with compasses. He shapes it in the form of man, of man in all his glory; that it may dwell in a shrine. He cut down cedars, or perhaps took a cypress or oak. He let it grow among the trees of the forest, or planted a pine, and the rain made it grow. It is man's fuel for burning; some of it he takes and warms himself, he kindles a fire and bakes bread.

But he also fashions a god and worships it; he makes an idol and bows down to it. Half of the wood he burns in the fire; over it he prepares his meal; he roasts his meat and eats his fill. He also warms himself and says, Ah, I am warm; I see the fire. From the rest he makes a god, his idol; he bows down to it and worships. He prays to it and says, Save me; you are my god. They know nothing, they understand nothing; their eyes are plastered over so they cannot see, and their minds closed so they cannot understand. No one stops to think, no one has the knowledge of understanding to say, half of it. I used for fuel; I even baked bread over it coals, I roasted meat, and I ate. Shall I make a detestable thing from what is left? Shall I bow down to a block of wood? He feeds on ashes, a deluded heart misleads him; he cannot save himself, or say, is not this thing in my right hand a lie? Remember these things, O Jacob, for you are my servant, O Israel. I have made you; you are my servant; O Israel, I will not forget you. I have swept away your offenses like a cloud, your sins like the morning mist. Return to me, for I have redeemed you. Sing for joy, O heavens, for the LORD has done this, shout aloud, O earth beneath. Burst into song, you mountains, you forests and all your trees, for the LORD has redeemed Jacob, he displays his glory in Israel. This is what the LORD says – your Redeemer, who formed you in the womb: I am the LORD, who has made all things, who alone stretched out the heavens, who spread out the earth by myself, who foils the signs of false prophets and makes fools of diviners, who overthrows the learning of the wise and turns it into nonsense.

Who carries out the words of his servants and fulfills the prediction of his messengers, who say of Jerusalem, it shall be inhabited, of the towns of Judah, they shall be built, and of their ruins, I will restore them, who says to the watery deep, Be dry, and I will dry up your streams, who says of Cyrus, He is my shepherd and will accomplish all that I please; he will say of Jerusalem, let it be rebuilt, and of the temple, let its foundations be laid." The Books of Enoch are special books that informed us about secret treasure's that stored in the heavens and speaks about the throne of God, the ruler, the elders, the clouds, the stars, snow and ice, the morning dew, and the great ocean that flooded the earth. Enoch, also described the Third Heaven – as the Mercy of Paradise and Justice of Hell, a place that is inconceivable pleasant and in the midst is the "Tree of Life." Enoch stated, this is where God the Father rests when He enter into "Paradise" a fine fragrance and more beautiful than any other heaven, it has an appearance of gold and crimson fire that covers the whole "Paradise" orchard trees and fruit trees that leads to the earth. Enoch says, there are many angels there singing and worshiping the Father, they looks after "Paradise" this place has been prepared for the righteous that suffer every kind of calamity in their life and for those whose soul have been afflicted and those who averted their eyes from injustice, those who carry out righteous judgment, who give bread to the hungry, those who cover their naked body with clothing, those who lift up the fallen, help the injured, this place has been prepared as an eternal inheritance.

And Enoch goes on to described more heavens; he stated that the northern region of heaven is a very frightful place, where all kinds of torture and torment take place the "Prison of Darkness" because there's no light and it's filled with rivers of black blazing fire everywhere and a very cruel place of detention with merciless angels carrying out instruction of torture without pity therefore this place is for those who don't glorify God the Father. According to the NIV Quiet Time Bible in 1 Corinthians 10:1-13 that says, "For I do not want you to be ignorant of the fact, brothers, that our forefathers were all under the cloud and that they all passed through the sea: They were all baptized into Moses in the cloud and in the sea, they all ate the same spiritual food and drank the same spiritual drink. For they drank from the spiritual rock that accompanied them, and that rock was the Messiah *(and this was the reason that God got mad at Moses, because he struck the "Rock").* Nevertheless, God was not pleased with most of them; their bodies were scattered over the desert, now these things occurred as examples to keep us from setting our hearts on evil things as they did. Do not be idolaters, as some of them were as it is written; the people sat down to eat and drink and got up to indulge in pagan revelry. We should not commit sexual immorality, as some of them did – and, in one day, twenty-three thousand died. We should not test God, as some of them did – and were killed by snakes. And do not grumble, as some of them did – and were killed by the destroying angel.

These things happened to them as examples and were written down as warnings for us, on whom the fulfillment of the ages has come. So, if you think you are standing firm, be careful that you don't fall! No temptation has seized you except what is common to man. And God is faithful; he will not let you be tempted beyond what you can bear. But when you are tempted, he will also provide a way out so that you can stand up under it." In the First Book of Enoch Ch. 80:1 that says, "And in those days the angel Uriel answered and said to me: Behold, I have shown thee everything, Enoch, and I have revealed everything to thee that thou shouldst see, this sun and this moon and the leaders of the stars of the heaven(s) and all those who turn them, their tasks and times and departures."

Believe it or not!

The Holy Spirit is the - Spirit of God and She is our Spiritual Mother. The second person of the Holy Trinity and the third person of the Holy Trinity is the Angel of God – our Spiritual Brother – the Messiah - the Son of God. It was He that made our yoke easier: According to Matthew 19:17-19, Do not murder, Do not commit adultery, Do not steal, Do not give false testimony, Honor your Father and Mother, *(As Above So Below)* and Love you neighbor as yourself. However, generation after generation we have lost understanding of our obligation to God the Father, and have taken His Laws, Commandments, Covenants, Feasts, Sabbaths and His Jubilees for granted.

Therefore, we forgot how to set ourselves aside from the "Nicolaitans" and we have forgotten that Christianity was forced on our ancestors, but today some of us – Black African American, are proud to call ourselves Christian. Thanks to the mercy of our Messiah, because we are all covered by His Blood; the Son of the Living God. The New Testament is for the Gentiles (from: Acts to Philemon) and if we take the Black race out of Christianity, then we will find our true God in the Old Testament – Adonai, El-Adonai (LORD), Adonai Elohai (The LORD My God), El, Eloah, Elohai, Elohiym (God), Qodesh L'Yahuah (Holiness to the LORD), El Elohiym (The Mighty God), El Shaddai (God Almighty), El Elyon, Elohiym Elyon (The Most High God), El Olam, Elohai Olam (The Everlasting God), Mashiach (The Messiah).

CHAPTER TEN
The Awakening

This study was done at Utah State University, on the level of international studies about – Nations, States and Nation-States: This study go on with the remarks by saying the terms for nation, state, and nation-state are frequently misuse because states are defined by sovereignty over a territory and a group of people and commonly call countries and each person has a sense of attachment to that nation. Nationalism takes the shared sense of attachment to a particular nation and uses it to justify for a political action, and the studies says: Nations generate identity and loyalty! They are named groups who share common histories, myths, culture, economy, rights and ethnic groups which have a common ancestry also solidarity within the group. But they do not engage in the politics of nationalism. Americans are encouraged to sing the national anthem rather than the state anthem in order to become more integrated with the idea of a nation. Even though it should be called the state anthem; a nation-state would be a sovereign territory with one group of individuals who share a common history *(What about Black People or African American?)*. But, today, a true nation-state in the academic sense of the world does not exist, but nearly every state or country in the world contains more than one national group.

The definition of "Place" included a form of identity; how people view the place in which they live, or their sense of attachment to a larger place meaning national identity which is builds upon the definition, and applies it to a specific nation. Namely, it is the idea that each person has a sense of attachment to a nation, in other words, they feel as though they belong to one nation more than any other. This attachment is formed by living in that nation and doing everyday things that support the existence of that nation – for example; paying taxes, maintaining national armed forces, celebrating national holidays, and cheering on national teams in the Olympic Games or the World Cup. These types of actions create a sense of belonging, or identity, for a nation's citizen. So, a person who has grown up in the United States attending the Fourth of July Celebrations, cheering for the United States' Olympic team, memorizing the national anthem, are most likely has developed an American national identity! So, why Black American citizens are call African American? And not just identify ourselves as American citizen, or Hebrew American?) However, this is just my "opinion" and another is, why was Malcolm X, assassinated? Was its because he was fighting for Black people identity; when he was talking about – Nationalism. Nationalism takes the shared sense of attachment to a particular nation and uses it to justify political action meaning – Nationalism is the belief that every nation has a right to control a piece of territory, basically, if a group of people has a shared sense of nationalism.

Meaning it loyalty and devotion to a nation exalting one nation above all others and placing primary emphasis on its culture and interests. Utah State University International Studies, stated: That the ideology of nationalism claims that a nation is not complete without territory. It also says that the geopolitical situation is unjust, or unfair, if a nation does not have or is not allowed to have its own territory. Many people use nationalism to justify conflict, as each nation fights for its right to a territory in which to live and govern. For example: The United States of America was formed when a group of people had a shared sense of belonging (nationalism) that was separate from the government they lived under (the British Crown). They fought, using their shared nationalism as the justification, to gain control of a territory; to call their own state, or country, and ultimately they were able to gain their territory and form a state that reflected their sense of nationalism. This is not a rally cry for nationalism! But a cry to find the concept of what is true. And what is not true. Because if we're not Gentile, then, who we are? And why are we still calling ourselves - African American? And why are we identifying ourselves as two nations then asked for one of those nation to pay reparation. The continent of African was our ancestor prison before they arrive here in America. When we read the Bible, we are reading about "Black Biblical History" a point of origin of the Black Hebrew Nation, that our God, scattered to the four corners of the earth. We often find ourselves confused about our point of origin of the truth, and the purpose of why our Messiah was born.

It was to restore the Garden of Eden and to rescue the children of Adam's and to save the lost nation of God and redemption for "All" who believe in the Son of the living God. From the beginning, Satan's purpose was to overthrow God's Kingdom and sit on His throne by deceitfulness and this is how Satan got mankind to transgress against our God. Which meant mankind was found guilty. And this is the reason mankind needed a Savior: According to the NIV Quiet Time Bible in Galatians 5:13-15 that says, "You, my brothers, were called to be free: But do not use your freedom to indulge the sinful nature, rather, serve one another in love. The entire law is summed up in a single command: Love your neighbor as yourself. If you keep on biting and devouring each other, watch out or you will be destroyed by each other." If we take the word "Love" and replace it with the word "Respect" we will get a better understanding of what God, is trying to teach us even though God do not need any help when He speak because His "Word" was with Him in the beginning. The Galatian Celts retained their culture at first, continuing to observe their ancient religious festivals and rituals but gradually became Hellenized to the point that they were referred to as "Greek-Gauls" by some Latin writers. They were conquered by Rome in 189 BCE, becoming a client state, but were granted a degree of autonomy under the reign of Deiotarus (the Divine Bull, r.c. 105 to 42 BCE) after Pompey the Great (1. c. 106-44 BCE) defeated Mithridates VI (r. 120-63 BCE) of Pontus in 63 BCE and was later absorbed into the Roman Empire in 25 BCE by Augustus Caesar.

It is best known from the biblical book of Galatians, a letter written to the Christian community there by Paul the Apostle. When the Apostle Paul, went to the City of Galatians, teaching the Gentiles and Jews about the Good News of the Spirit of Truth and Righteousness – which is the Holy Spirit. He was not overlooking the Law of Moses. But he was delivering them from condemnation of the law into Grace and Mercy, so they could walk with the Spirit of God. Even today, we must submit to circumcision of the heart and change the way we think meaning – repent. This was the message that the Apostle Paul, was teaching and to be more particular, circumcision of the heart implies to humility, faith, hope and charity more or less, a right judgment of ourselves confident but not arrogant, cleanses of the mind that is far from perfection, cut off vain thoughts, and that we are not sufficient of ourselves to help ourselves because with the Spirit of God, we can do anything. That it is God, alone who "work" in us by his almighty power, the Holy Spirit. Either to will or to do good; it's impossible for us even to think a good thought without the supernatural assistance of the "Holy Spirit" as to "Create" ourselves, or to "Renew" our "Soul" in righteousness and true holiness. And what Paul was dealing with by bringing in a new way of thinking into an old legalistic lifestyle, is no different than what we are dealing with today; this is why we must break away from – traditions.

According to the NIV Quiet Time Bible in Galatians 5:16-18 that says, "So I say, live by the spirit, and you will not gratify the desires of the sinful nature: For the sinful nature desires what is contrary to the Spirit and the Spirit what is contrary to the sinful nature. They are in conflict with each other, so that you do not do what you want. But if you are led by the Spirit, you are not under *(the)* law." We have the freedom, to have a relationship with God without requirements but to enter into the church of Christ, there is a ceremony called – Baptism. When a person is immersed in water symbolize their sin being washed away brought back from the death into a new life by faith in Christ, and now He is the savior of our soul. According to Matthew 28:18-20 that says, "Then Jesus came to them and said, "All authority in heaven and on earth has been given to me. Therefore, go and make disciples of all nations, baptizing them in the name of the Father and of the Son and of the Holy Spirit, and teaching them to obey everything I have commanded you. And surely, I am with you always, to the very end of the age." However, the conflict we are dealing with is call – Libertinism, it's not a political party but a lifestyle of behavior characterized by self-indulgence, lack of restraint, especially involving in sexual promiscuity and the rejection of God's moral authority by falling into a trap design by Satan himself. Please, watch the YouTube channel called: Howard Pittman's Near Death Experience.

Our Heavenly Father welcomes all society misfits into His Kingdom: Because no one is perfect. The summation of the law demanded is love, and then replace it with the word respect so it can read like this; respect your neighbor as yourself. And when we do this we are fulfilling the whole law. But remember; the only requirement to enter into the church of Christ is – Baptism. Believing in God the Father, and the Son of God, we will receive the Holy Spirit. Then by the Living Water, we have the power to walk with the Spirit of God. It's not all about being perfect or criticizing other believers for falling short from living their best life but we should encourage one another to do better, because a legalistic environment will condemn a person to the lake of fire or the prison of darkness, by having unlawful ways. The founder of the Legalistic school was Hsun Tzu or Hsun-tzu – the most important principle in his thinking was that humans are inherently evil, and inclined toward criminal and selfish behavior. Thus, if humans are allowed to engage in their natural proclivities, the result will be conflict and social disorder. Understand this: Throughout world history, the name of the Messiah has been changed in order to change the skin color of the person that gave the message of "Repent" because it is He that bringing a New Nation. And today we are still not understanding the message. According to the NIV Quiet Time Bible in Romans 8:1-4 says, "Therefore, there is now no condemnation for those who are in Christ Jesus, because through the law of the Spirit of Life set me free from the law of sin and death.

For what the law was powerless to do in that it was weakened by the sinful nature, God did by sending his own Son in the likeness of sinful man to be a sin offering. And so, he condemned sin in the sinful man, in order that the righteous requirements of the law might be fully met in us, who do not live according to the sinful nature but according to the Spirit." All believers of the Church of Christ have an obligation to the Law of the Spirit. Which is incredibly better, incredibly effective and incredibly powerful than the Old Law. Because everything is written on our heart, and we have to volunteer to keep them and Honor our Spiritual Mother and our Spiritual Father. According to Jeremiah 31:31-40 that says, "The time is coming, declares the LORD, when I will make a new covenant with the House of Israel and with the House of Judah: It will not be like the covenant I made with their forefathers when I took them by the hand to lead them out of Egypt, because they broke my covenant, though I was a husband to them, declares the LORD. This is the covenant I will make with the House of Israel after that time, declares the LORD. I will put my law in their minds and write it in their hearts. I will be their God, and they will be my people. No longer will a man teach his neighbor or a man his brother *(sister)*, saying, know the LORD, because they will all know me, from the least of them to the greatest, declares the LORD. For I will forgive their wickedness and will remember their sins no more. This is what the LORD says, he who appoints the sun to shine by day, who decrees the moon and stars to shine by night, who stirs up the sea so that its waves roar – the LORD Almighty is his name.

Only if these decrees vanish from my sight, declares the LORD, will the descendants of Israel ever cease to be a nation before me. This is what the LORD says: Only if the heavens above can be measured and the foundations of the earth below be searched out will I reject all the descendants of Israel, because of all they have done, declares the LORD. The days are coming, declares the LORD, when this city will be rebuilt for me from the Tower of Hananel to the Corner Gate. The measuring line will stretch from there straight to the hill of Gareb and then turn to Goah. The whole valley where dead bodies and ashes are thrown, and all the terraces out to the Kidron Valley on the east as far as the corner of the Horse Gate, will be holy to the LORD. The city will never again be uprooted or demolished." We cannot even imagine the love that our God has for His children especially when we come in faith, accepting His Son, as our personal Savior and get baptize with that water ceremony confessing our belief only then the Spirit of the Law writes God's Law on our hearts. Only than we are born again able to walk with the Spirit of God. The Old Testament law gave us a standard of keeping the law, but the New Testament law gave us the desire, the power, the ability to walk and listen to the Law of the Spirit. For: She is the comforter and the helper. The Law of the Spirit - She is our Comforter, our Helper – We are a fleshly creature that has the desires of the flesh and material things of this world, but right now, we need your guidance, your essential truth and righteousness to direct my decisions. To govern my thoughts because the race that I'm running is called; life or death.

185

The Old Law cannot find me guilty any more but by my decisions alone can bring eternal death or eternal life upon my soul. So, we desperately need the Holy Spirit to remind us of the commandment of our Messiah daily, Matthew 19:16-19, and write them on our heart. I know that walking with the Spirit of the Law, is a constant battle with the trends of this world. If I don't follow trends of this world, I will become a social misfit around my friends and family, then, so let it be! This is why we need your Comforter and your Helper – the Spirit of God upon our life that will allow us to pursue a spiritual lifestyle serving God the Father daily. And with your own words God, it's you that's reminding us that being a friend to this world is an enemy to you! And this is why the Holy Spirit have to remind us to be passionate about His Spirit. That He place in us and that we should be faithful to Her. Also, the Scriptures says: That You oppose the proud but gives grace to the humble, so we should humble ourselves before the Holy Spirit, and resist the devil and he will flee. And it's you that reminds us to come closer to you, and wash our hands and purify our heart, for loyalty is divided between us and you, Heavenly Father. Therefore, it's not our heart that needs your help but it's our mind that need to stop chasing after bad habits running after the flesh and material things which can bring death to our spirit by living in the moment. So, we need your helper to find a soulmate suitable to our spirit and not to our flesh. Give us the desire, the will, and the ability to walk in your good pleasure and to live a life according to your will and the Spirit of the Law. Help us to live under the covenant that is set by you and we ask this in the Authority of your Son. Also - Amen come from "Amein."

Which in Hebrew means: Honest, Faithful, and Trustworthy. And Amen, is derived from the Hebrew word – Amein, which means; certainty, truth and verily. Amen - is found in the King James Bible, and both the Old and the New Testament – can be expressed in endless ways, from a soft whisper, to a joyous shout. Another thing: That's importat to talk about which happens outside of God's covenant of marriage, which is a sinful act that can bring death through sexual immorality, sexual misconduct, impure sexual misconduct and this is called – Fornication. However, spiritual adultery is worse than physical adultery because the person is following idols, worshiping other gods and demonstrating unfaithfulness to God the Father. It's having an undue fondness for the things of the world: According to the NIV Quiet Time Bible in Jeremiah 3:20 that says, "But like a woman unfaithful to her husband, so you have been unfaithful to me, O House of Israel." The Bible tells us that people who choose to be friends with the world are an adulterous people having enmity against God – according to James 4:4-5 that says, "You adulterous people, don't you know that friendship with the world is hatred toward God? Anyone who chooses to be a friend of the world become an enemy of God. Or do you think Scripture says without reason that the Spirit – He caused to live in us envies intensely?" It's like an adultery husband wants his wife and another lover claiming to love God, while cultivation friendship with the world. Today most Christian yet to find their true love for God and this is the direct opposites of the will of Satan because he want to captivate our mind by giving us the pleasures of the world.

187

Influence us with comfort like financial security or so-called freedom to do whatever we pleased as long we don't repent! Apostasy must be called what it is "Spiritual Adultery" and all of us are marked by this in some way or the other. Because the whole Western Christian Religion has been undercut by liberal theology. If we (Christian) take the time and look at some of our Cinema, TV shows, Music, even in some of our Churches, we should be saying "Woe, O you liberal society and churches where is the Gospel of Grace, being preached? According to the passage and according to what has been written. Are we saddened on what we see and hear? Where is the loyalty to the living God? The Judge of the Universe – the only adequate Bridegroom for all the people in the world. We know and have seem how desperately wrong and sinful physical adultery is; but notice that our Messiah gave us priority in Matthew 21:28-32 that says, "What do you think? There was a man who had two sons(daughters). He went to the first and said, Son(Daughter), go and work today in the vineyard. I will not, he(she) answered, but later he(she) changed his(her) mind and went. Then the father went to the other son(daughter) and said the same thing. He(She) answered, I will sir, but he(she) did not go. Which of the two did what his father wanted? The first, they answered! Jesus said to them, I tell you the truth, the tax collectors and the prostitutes are entering the kingdom of God ahead of you. For John came to you to show you the way of righteousness, and you did not believe him. But the tax collectors and the prostitutes did, and even after you saw this, you did not repent and believe him."

He was speaking to the religious leaders of his days: The Messiah is not minimized liberal theology, but He is telling the religious leaders who have turned away from external authority of the coming Kingdom of God the Father. He reminds us that the harlots and those who had collected taxes for the Romans will go into the Kingdom of God before them: The Holy Spirit - is trying to remind us that sexual sin is sinful, but spiritual adultery is even worse. There used to be a time when participating in some sexual activities was frowned upon but not anymore, sexual behavior is becoming increasingly popular with people without any shame. Today, sexual activities are actually celebrated and the devil himself has been quietly working to deceive God's children in ways that's cunning and misleading especially when he uses the entertainment industry like movies, music, theater and all forms of social media that's available to dismantle godly values relating to sex. For the safety of our mental status and our salvation the people who by God's Grace belong to Him: We who are in Christ's, who have been redeemed, on the basis of the blood of the Lamb – let us understand that we are now called to take one more crucial step. Because we are save according to the New Law of our Messiah – and we are now His bride. And what does our divine Bridegroom want from us?

He wants not only doctrinal faithfulness but He want us show love for one another day by day – not in theory mind but in practice in the midst of this unfaithfulness world. The devil has built some kind of scheme that sex outside of marriage is no longer a sin. He has convinced God's children that we shouldn't have any shame if we participate in sex before marriage. And some people may think, if we are not have any sex that something is wrong with that person which is not true! The devil is trying to normalize fornication and physical adultery by having us to overlook the side effects of sin. We don't know what evil we're opening up just by having sexual pleasures. Sex is a spiritual act designed by God in order for mankind to multiply on the face of the earth and create something that's good but the devil used sex for something that is evil and trap us in a situation that we may not be ready for – parenthood. According to the NIV Quiet Time Bible in Genesis 2:24 that says, "For this reason a man will leave his father and mother and be united to his wife, and they will become one flesh." So when a man and woman that are not married decide to have sex they are breaking a Spiritual Law. Also this is why God said: It's a "Abomination" when the same gender come together and have a sexual relaxtionship because they cannot create, plus they do not represent the image of God. God's was not being repressive and cruel, limiting our sexual behavior between a man and a woman: He was/is protecting mankind from spiritual attacks from the dark power, principalities and the rulers of hate, fear, and destruction that can enter into our lives through the spiritual realm of wickedness.

There are many things that God has been telling His children "Do not" because of the punishment that is attached to them and when we "Do Them" we "sinned" because we just broke His commanded in His judicial system. According to the NIV Quiet Time Bible in Luke 12:47-49 that says, "That servant who knows his master's will and does not get ready or does not do what his master wants will be beaten with many blows. But the one who does not know and does things deserving punishment will be beaten with few blows. From everyone who has been given much, much will be demanded; and from the one who has been entrusted with much, much more will be asked." For example: Telling a lie is a sin, and it's outside the body, and will not effected body. However, the only sin committed that will effected the body is "Adultery or Fornication" sexual immorality it's a sin that will effected the body and some form or other. According to 1 Corinthians 6:16-20 that says, "Do you not know that he who unites himself with a prostitute is one with her in body? For it is said, the two will become one flesh. But he who unites himself with the Lord is one with him in spirit. Flee from sexual immorality. All other sins a man commits are outside his body, but he who sins sexually sins against his own body. Do you not know that your body is a temple of the Holy Spirit, who is in you, whom you have received from God? You are not your own; you were bought at a price. Therefore, Honor God (the Father) with your body." The devil has no problem setting up God's children with someone who has the potential to rod, steal, or kill a person soul by using sexual pleasures.

191

Again, I am not judging anyone because I'm guilty of sexual pleasures so I'm speaking from personal experience. Choosing the wrong partner in marriage or even in dating can be destructive and can actively separate you from God. However a few casual sexual relationships are not worth eternal death but in some cases physical death. There is no greater state of being than being in the presence of God. Without self-control, a person's desire will take a man or a woman captive and make them a slave to sexual pleasures. According to the NIV Quiet Time Bible in Judges 14:1-3 that says, "Samson went down to Timnah and saw there a young Philistine woman: When he returned, he said to his father and mother, I have seen a Philistine woman in Timnah; now get her for me as my wife. His father and mother replied, isn't there an acceptable woman among your relatives or among all our people? Must you go to the uncircumcised Philistines to get a wife? But Samson said to his father, get her for me: She's the right one for me." Drinking liquor especially in the night club's can leave us powerless and blind that can lead people into sexual immorality rather than fulfilling the purposes of God and can derail God's plans for our life – Samson is an example of this! According to the NIV Quiet Time Bible in 2 Timothy 4:1-5 that says, "In the presence of God and of Christ Jesus, who will judge the living and the dead, and in view of his appearing and his kingdom, I give you this charge: Preach the word; be prepared in season and out of season; correct, rebuke and encourage – with great patience and careful instruction.

For the time will come when man will not put up with sound doctrine, instead, to suit their own desires, they will gather around them a great number of teachers to say what their itching ears want to hear. They will turn their ears away from the truth and turn aside to myths. But you, keep your head in all situations, endure hardship do the work of an evangelist discharge all the duties of your ministry." Question: How do we know if our religious leaders are telling the congregation the whole truth and nothing but the truth so help them God? About the fall of man? The word "Utopian" is attached to the "Garden of Eden" for God created a man and a woman to live in prosperity and in unity with the creator. There in the garden was the Tree of life, the Tree of Knowledge of Good and Evil also the Serpent. Which the scripture identifies the Serpent as the Great Dragon – who is called the Devil or Satan, and his forked tongue signals the nature of deception but originally, he was the Moring Star of God before his fall from grace. According to Revelation 12:9 that says, "The great dragon was hurled down – that ancient serpent called the devil or Satan *(was an Archangel),* who leads the whole world astray: He was hurled to the earth, and his angels with him." And in Revelation 12:7-8 that says, "And there was war in heaven. Michael *(An Archangel)* and his angels fought against the dragon, and the dragon and his angels fought back. But he was not strong enough, and they lost their place in heaven."

193

And in Isaiah 14:12-15 that says, "How you have fallen from heaven, O morning star, son of the dawn *(Lucifer)*! You have been cast down to the earth, you who once laid low the nations! You said in your heart, I will ascend to heaven; I will raise my throne above the stars of God; I will sit enthroned on the mount of assembly, on the utmost heights of the sacred mountain. I will ascend above the tops of the clouds; I will make myself like the Most High. But you are brought down to the grave, to the depths of the pits." However, the attachment to the Tree of Life, was the fundamental desire of humanity to achiever perfection. This was Adam's mission but first he must obedient not to eat the Fruit of the Tree of the Knowledge of Good and Evil *(Or not to have sex with Eve).* According to the NIV Quiet Time Bible in Proverbs 11:30 that says, "The fruit of the righteous is a tree of life, and he who wins souls is wise." More of less to be a blessing to the person around you, and other words draw those around you closer to God's salvation. It was Adam job to learn how to "Love" Eve, without having sexual pleasures with her or to win her soul. This is where dating come in! Also in Proverbs 15:4 that says, "The tongue that brings healing is a tree of life, but a deceitful tongue crushes the spirit." In the Garden of Eden, the tree of life represents a righteous man filled with wisdom and the tree of knowledge of good and evil represents the ideal woman. This is why these two trees were planted next to each other in the center of the garden and only through the perfect man we are able to enter into the Kingdom of God.

So, if the ideal woman represents the tree of knowledge of good and evil: What did the fruit represents? But let us recognize we are not talking about a literal fruit because our Messiah said: In Matthew 15:11 that says, "What goes into a man's mouth does not make him unclean, but what comes out of his mouth, that is what makes him unclean." Furthermore, the original sin is not passed on throughout humanity by just eating a fruit, however the fruit symbolizes love on the sexual level. Spiritual Adultery – Adam, disobey God commandment "Do not" eat from the tree of knowledge of good and evil. According to Song of Song or Song of Solomon 4:12 that says, "You are a garden locked up, my sister, my bride; you are a spring enclosed, a sealed fountain." The civilization they brought forth was good and evil, however after the spiritual adultery - they discover that they were naked, and God clothed them with lambskin to hide the fruits of their bodies not their mouth. But if Eve claimed that Lucifer made her eat from the tree of knowledge of good and evil, this means that Lucifer had sex with Eve, yes, a fallen angel had sex with a human being who were both spiritual and a human being at that time. Even now when we have sex there is a physical component of sex and a spiritual component of sex and a emotional component of sex. And put all of these component together can be called metaphysics. So, Lucifer and Eve had a sexual relationship on a spiritual level and on a physical level. The fallen Eve from her spiritual level persuaded Adam to have sex with her on the spiritual level making Adam and Eve fall from their spiritual level and committing spiritual adultery breaking the commanded "Do Not."

According to the NIV Quiet Time Bible in Proverbs 30:20 that says, "This is the way of an adulteress: She eats and wipes her mouth and says, I've done nothing wrong." The fruit symbolizes love on a sexual level however Eve, should have become the ideal woman but through her guilty and the pain of her conscience she realized that her right companion was Adam, not Satan the Morning Star and this is how Satan had a claim over humanity by the fall of the Spiritual level to the physical level. And this correlated by the punishment of Eve/women, in their pains with childbirth and childbearing. This is just one man's theory that the fall of man was a sexual fall called "Spiritual Adultery" and not by the eating a apple.

CHAPTER ELEVEN
It's Not Over Yet

After the "Great Gathering" we're going to witness a reunion between the two Adam's: According to the NIV Quiet Time Bible in 1 Corinthians 15:45-47 that says, "So it is written; the first man Adam became living being and the last Adam, a life-giving spirit. The spiritual did not come first but the natural, and after that the spiritual. The first man was of the dust of the earth and the second man from heaven." The angels in the heavens will sing: Worthy, worthy to the lamb that was crucified and now "He live" everyone in heaven will bow down at the Messiah feet – Yahshua, (His Hebrew name): And worship the Son of God, praising him before the "Crystal Sea" that's in front of the throne of God the Father. Standing on Mount Zion we will see the 144,000 angels that were redeemed with the sound of water and thunder, holding in their hands "Harps" playing a new song's singing and worshipping in front of the throne of God: The song are dedicated to Moses and to the Messiah, a song of "Deliverance" for those who had passes through "Jacob's Trouble."

The intercessor – the Holy Spirit – our Spiritual Mother; will welcome "Her" children by saying: They have been delivered from famine, pestilence and they endured suffering but now they hunger and thirst for the truth, dressed in all white robes with no guilt, because they been washed in the blood of the Lamb. According to Revelation 7:1-17 that says, "After this I saw four angels standing at the four corners of the earth, holding back the four winds of the earth to prevent any wind from blowing on the land or on the sea or on any tree. Then I saw another angel coming up from the east, having the Seal of the Living God. He called out in a loud voice to the four angels who had been given power to harm the land and the sea: Don't harm the land or the sea or the trees until we put a Seal on the foreheads of the servants of our God. Then I heard the number of those who were sealed: 144,000 from all the Tribes of Israel.

- From the Tribe of Judah 12,000 were sealed.

- From the Tribe of Reuben 12,000

- From the Tribe of Gad 12,000

- From the Tribe of Asher 12,000

- From the Tribe of Naphtali 12,000

- From the Tribe of Manasseh 12,000

- From the Tribe of Simeon 12,000

- From the Tribe of Levi 12,000

- From the Tribe of Issachar 12,000

- From the Tribe of Zebulun 12,000

- From the Tribe of Joseph 12,000

- From the Tribe of Benjamin 12,000

After this I looked and there before me was a great multitude that no one could count, from every nation, tribe, people and language, standing before the Throne, and in front of the Lamb. They were wearing white robes and were holding palm branches in their hands. And they cried out in loud voice:

Salvation belongs to our God,

Who sits on the Throne, and to the Lamb.

All the angels were standing around the Throne, and around the Elders and the Four Living Creatures. They fell down on their faces before the Throne, and worshiped God, saying: Amen! Praise, Glory, Wisdom, Thanks, Honor, Power and Strength, be to our God, forever and ever. Amen! Then one of the Elders asked me: These in white robes – who are they? And where did they come from? I answered, Sir, you know. And he said, these are they who have come out of the Great Tribulation: They have washed their robes and made them white in the blood of the Lamb. Therefore, they are before the Throne of God, and serve him day and night in his Temple, and He who sits on the Throne will spread his tent over them. Never again will they hunger, never again will they thirst. The sun will not beat upon them, nor any scorching heat. For the Lamb at the center of the Throne, will be their shepherd: He will lead them to Springs of Living Water.

And God will wipe away every tear from their eyes." O' House of Israel, this is the time that we must search all the Scriptures for the truth! It's time we become wise, we have a Savior, and our loss of memory is not going to count against God's children, but the path to the Holy Sanctuary: Is narrow (Tradition vs. Scripture). However everyone is not going to pass through because it's not about going to church or volunteering to give money. We cannot buy our way into heaven therefore we have an obligation to keep the Messiah Commandments and allowed the Spirit of Law: Lead our life. God gave His children deeds to freed our spirit to led His children into a New Law. But how can we identify ourselves when we don't really know who we are! The Spanish and Portuguese Jews are our ancestors from the Tribe of Judah, Benjamin and Levi, our proof come from - Hannah Adams (October 2, 1755 – December 15, 1831), she was an American author of books on comparative religion in the United States. Ms. Adams was born in Medford, Massachusetts and she was the first woman in the U.S., who worked professionally as a writer – one of her books was called: The History of the Jews – From the Destruction of Jerusalem to the Present Time. Ms. Adams was the cousin of the U.S. President John Adams also a member of the Anthology Club of the President. And had freedom to view his private library in his home at Quincy, Massachusetts. An encyclopedic and balanced treatment of world religions at a time when such a thing did not exist in the fledgling United States. And she also authored other widely books volumes on religion history and campaigned for the first copyright law passed in this nation.

We can quote from her book and conclude that the Spanish and Portuguese slaves are originally from the Tribe of Judah, Benjamin and Levi. This fact along connects African American to the name "Negro" because this name along is our evidence for a case for "Reparation" and denying this word is denying who we truly are! The House of Israel and the House of Judah, never been lost! We have always lived in this country before it became the United States of America, and the Book of Mormon is our evidence of this fact! And we should not forget about our brother and sister who died in the journey crossing the Atlantic Ocean, coming to this land; again this is just one man's opinion! The only way to ask for reparations legally is: If we bring each state to civil court because of a crime that already been committed and experience generations and generations of Racial Disparities, and Jim Crow Laws – which was an unwritten law against American Citizens. With policies and regulations that was in violations of human rights for Black American Citizens. We were segregation based on our skin color and this country violated our 13th, 14th and 15th Amendment of the Constitution of the United States of America. This refers to the circumstances when people are injured in the course of their employment: That help this nation to become as great. They're automatically, by law, entitled to workers' compensation benefits, which is a portion of their lost wages, and were entitled to any medical expenses that are related to the accident (i.e., in the pursue of liberty).

We know that these people who committed these violent acts are no longer living, but their relatives or descendants are reaping the benefits of wealth from free labor of slavery, and we can added this to the violation legacy of Black Domestic Terrorists - against Black Negroes Citizens. In the pursuit of Happiness, Liberty and Freedom – which is a part of the Constitution of the United States of America. It's a shame and this country should be embarrass for the humane treatment of one of her citizens. Which is a crime against humanity also the Federal Government is still liable for pulling the Union Soldiers from the Southern States that help created the KKK – White Supremacist Citizens. With pure conscious added pain and suffering to life of Black American citizens and destroying their properties which could had created generational wealth for Black American citizen. But instead Black American citizens lost important families valuables and members these crimes are embedded in Black America History.

And what are the steps for making a third-party lawsuit?

1. Identifying the liable party:

2. Uncovering relevant insurance policies:

3. Calculating the damages owed to the plaintiff:

4. Creating an injury claim:

5. Filing the complaint in pursuit of compensation:

One of our last Black Civil Rights Leader, who was willing to challenge the United States of America for "Reparations" was Dr. Martin Luther King Jr., prior to his assassination he was trying to organize his second march on Washington D.C., with this question on his mind "Where is our money?" If the defending party does not accept the liability and does not want to pay a fair settlement to the claimant, then the claim needs to be escalated as a lawsuit. At this point: The lawsuit should be prepared and filed with the correct court, which will eventually set a court date to hear the legal contest. Before the trial – there will be a discovery process that allows both sides to review the evidence and potentially negotiate of settlement. Assuming no settlement is possible, the third-party lawsuit will continue, and the trial will commence. An argument will be brought before the court in some form, about a jury which is: *(The History of Violence Against Black American Citizens).* This evidence will be used to try and reach a verdict but in some cases in front of a judge. By the end of the trial, a verdict will be decided. If it favors the plaintiff – the court or the jury will decide a fair amount of compensation, it can be challenged or reduced based on the state or federal damage caps. Theologian: George Eldon Ladd, said: "The root ideal in "Justification" is the Declaration of God, the righteous "Judge" that the man who believes in God, sinful though he may be (or) is righteous, is viewed as being righteous because (of) God, he has come into a righteous relationship with God. However, properly understanding justification has to do with God Declaration, about the sinner.

It has nothing to do with the sinner but about holiness, which occurs with sanctification, which is related to but distinct from justification. However, the whole world was given a gift of justification through sanctification by faith in the Son of God – we know this: But can Black and Brown citizens overlook the crisis that led to the long suffering of economics and the breakdown in the families, what about the incarceration of Black and Brown men and women which led to the wealth for investors. What about the prison system? What about the mental illness and the psychological trauma from slavery? And how can politics address the racial inequity for reparations? At the Harvard Kennedy School Institution of Politics, there was a platform discussion about this topic with Professor Cornell William Brooks and Professor Linda J. Bilmes to argue: Reparations for Black Americans – Radical or Routine? This is a must watch YouTube Channel to view with groundbreaking research argument called: Is the government responsible for economics and social injustice to pay compensation for socioeconomic injustice for Black Americans? The conversation is about reparations and has been going on for a while behind the scenes but the calls for reparations are getting louder. Another, YouTube video to watch is called: The Arc of Justice: Reparations for African Americans – which speaks about race in public policies on social justice and injustice. This platform that place at the University of Illinois Institution for Research on Race and Public Polices. Also be sure to watch the YouTube Channel called: Reparations for Slavery – The Role of Repentance in Politics.

A heart stopping presentation about racism and the impact it had on Black people, especially after the Union Army left the Southern States in 1877. But why is reparation important? Because it's a means to acknowledge and repair the causes and consequences of human rights violations and inequality that happen in this country emerging from racial injustice. In the Brookings Report: Why we need reparations for Black Americans; by Rashawn Ray and Andre M. Perry, written in April 15, 2020, they argued: That all victims of human rights violations have a right to reparations and it's important to remember that compensation or payment of money is just one form of addressing economic separation of wealth, other ways include but are not limited to the restitution of civil injustice, political rights, physical rehabilitation for mental illness and granting access to business loans, fair housing, fair health care and education. Saying: These added policies may work to close the gap of wealth with the help of the federal government, state institutions and non-state organizations may find a way to meet the needs of the descendants of Negros Slavery. To implement a reparations program to narrow the scope of wealth. The White Supremacists - whose ancestor are still alive today in the 21st Century, are reaping the benefits of wealth and building opportunities in their communities meanwhile, in the Black communities we are still struggling to catch up and with the average White families have roughly ten times the amount of wealth than the average Black families.

There should be an need to address this racial disparities in wealth here in America, however, still today the United States has not yet, compensated the descendants of enslaved Black Americans for the free labor which the valued was over $3 billion dollars back in 1860's and the value placed on cotton alone was about $250 million dollars. And this fueled the economy back than for the United States, so answer this question? Does the federal government need to atone for this hardship? Absolutely! The fact is this: White high school drop-outs have more wealth and opportunities for wealth than a Black college graduate here in America. And did you know this; the Japanese American were paid $1.5 billion dollars for those injured during World War II, even the Jews received reparations for the Holocaust with the help of the Marshall Plan. Black Americans are the only group of people who did not received reparations for racial disparities and legacies of discrimination meanwhile White Americans have the ability to accrue tremendous wealth and opportunities. We cannot forget about our enslaved ancestors that died on the journey to America, and we're talking about millions of Black people from the Tribes of Judah, Benjamin and Levi. Throughout history in this great country called, America – Black American citizens have suffer great lost because of racial disparities. We have fought in the Civil War and won, but less than a year after General William Sherman's order the Field Order 15, that each Black family should receive forty 40 acres and a mule. It was reversed by the President Andrew Johnson, intervened, and ordered that the vast majority of confiscated land be returned to its former owners.

This included most of the land that freedmen had settled on but the Federal government dispossessed tens of thousands of Black landholders in Georgia and South Carolina, even though some black fought back, driving away former owners. The federal troops evicted them by force, so, the Federal Government played a major part in discrimination and racial disparities for Black American citizens. Still today, Black and Brown citizens have fought in all of the wars, helping this great country to maintain the status of being the greatest military in the world. On March 10, 2020, Rashawn Ray highlighted historical data on slavery and why there is a racial wealth gap between White and Black American Citizens: He testified in front of the Maryland General Assembly's Health and Government Operations Committee on House Bill 1201 to establish a Maryland Reparations Commission for the establishment of the Harriet Tubman Community Investment Act. This is something that every state legislature in the United States should be following with one harmony pushing for this bill. Mr. Ray's example of informing the court about the legacy of slavery in his state that allowed for reparations for descendants of enslaved Negro Americans. And would help atone for racial disparities, and it would help with the racial wealth gap damages that should have been awarded. Over a historic time period of policies and practices harmed for the Black American citizens, in the pursuit of life, liberty and happiness to live the American Dream – therefore please read: Mr. Ray's full testimony it's a must read.

Many of the most famous building in the United States were built by enslaved people including the White House also the U.S. Capitol Building and rebuilt it again after the war of 1812. Our ancestors also helped build the Trinity Church in New York's Financial District and many of the buildings on Wall Street. Thomas Jefferson's entire property was built by Black slaves and the Georgetown University's campus were built by enslaved people, not to mention Harvard University Law School, which were built by enslave people and there's are other institutions that our ancestors built that standing in front of faces today like! The Statue of Freedom on top of the Capitol was made by Philip Reid, an enslaved person but by the time the statue was set on the roof of the capitol in 1863, Mr. Reid was a free man since the Emancipation Bill was passed in 1862. The Smithsonian Institution, were built between 1847 and 1855, is made from red sandstone, which was quarried by enslaved people but didn't work on the actual building, however the Fraunces Tavern, one of the oldest buildings in Manhattan, and New York's first prison and hospital were built by enslaved people. Faneuil Hall was built in 1740s – known as the "Cradle of Liberty" this spot is popular for both tourists and politicians giving speeches. It was named after Peter Faneuil, an owner and trader of enslaved people, which was bolstered by money he made off slavery. Based in Charleston Harbor in South Carolina, Fort Sumter is an artificial island that was built in 1892 – from bricks that were made by enslaved people and in 1864, during the Civil War.

The Confederate Army made enslaved people repair the fortress while it was under attack, the Castillo de San Marcos. Which is the oldest masonry fort in the U.S., was built in part by enslaved Native Americans, for Spanish forces. They worked in tough conditions for about 25 years in the 17th century to build the fortress. The University of North Carolina at Chapel Hill is the oldest public university in the country, built in 1793 – it harnessed slave labor to build many of its early structures. Thomas Jefferson's Monticello home in Charlottesville was built by enslaved people, and in 2014, former President Barrack Obama took former French President Francois Hollande on a tour and said the house represented the U.S. complicated history with slavery. Including Jefferson's ties to it, despite helping to draft the Declaration of Independence, now, what do you think about the 4th of July? Negro slaves have built some major infrastructures in the United States from the ground up, and this was off of free labor! Remember, slavery was just abolished around 158 years ago no other group of people can say that they built, what Black people built in this country. And no other group of people can say, they have dealt with so much domestic terrorism than Black people. There's a must watch YouTube channel called: Democracy Now! By: Ta-Nehisi Coates - Reparations Are Not Just About Slavery But Also Centuries Of Theft.

Wallace Stanciel

According to the NIV Quiet Time Bible in Proverbs 6:16-20 that says, "There are six things the LORD hates, seven that are detestable to him: Haughty eyes, a lying tongue, hands that shed innocent blood, a heart that devises wicked schemes, feet that are quick to rush into evil, a false witness who pours out lies and a man who stirs up dissension among brothers. My son, keep your father's commands and do not forsake your mother's teaching." (Here! Again evidence that the Holy Spirit – is our Spiritual Mother). The 14th Amendment – reminds us by saying that all persons born or naturalized in the United States are subject to the jurisdiction (a system of law and courts), wherein they reside. No, state shall make or enforce any law which shall abridge the privileges or immunities of citizens of the United States; nor shall any state deprive any person of life, liberty, or property, without due process of (the) law nor deny to any person within its jurisdiction the equal protection of the laws. After the Civil War, the Negro became citizens their Constitution under the Equal Protection of the law got violated: The same amendment that liberated them to express their liberty and freedom in the pursuit of happiness as American citizens was breached. The 14th Amendment has been breached as we witnessed the survivors of the "Tulsa Race Massacre" are appealing a judge's decision to dismiss their case for reparations.

CNN – reporter (Justin Gamble and Christina Maxouris, updated 2:23 AM EDT, Tuesday July 11, 2023), that the last three known survivors of the Tulsa Race Massacre – one of the country's deadliest acts of racial violence – will appeal a judge's recent decision to dismiss their lawsuit seeking reparations to the state Supreme Court, their attorneys announced. Lessie Benning field Randle, 108, Viola Fletcher, 109, and her brother, Hughes Van Ellis, 102, had been locked in a years-long legal battle with the City of Tulsa and other officials over opportunities taken from them when the city's Greenwood neighborhood – dubbed "Black Wall Street" – was burned to the ground by a violent White mob in 1921. Judge - Caroline Wall, dismissed the case on that Friday: An statement read by attorney Damario Solomon-Simmons during a Monday news conference – we were forced to plead this case beyond what is required under Oklahoma standards, which is certainly a familiar circumstance when Black American citizens ask the American legal system to work for them, and now, Judge Wall has condemned us to languish on Oklahoma's appellate docket, the three survivors said in a statement read by their attorney – like so many Black Americans, we carry the weight of intergenerational racial trauma day in and day out. The dismissal of this case is just one more example of how America's and specifically Tulsa's, legacy of racial harm, racial distress is disproportionally and unjustly borne by Black communities – we will not rest until there's justice for Greenwood.

During the news conference, Solomon-Simmons said; they found out about the judge's decision Friday night and called it an unexpected and hurtful, difficult blow. We will be moving forward with an appeal on this case to the Oklahoma Supreme Court, the attorney said; adding they're also calling on the federal government to investigate the massacre. This generational injustice, yesterday, today and tomorrow will be met by generational rights. We ain't going nowhere, "the lawmaker added." Each state of the United States of America - is responsible for their jurisdiction therefore some type of reparations should be awarded for the violent acts against their Black citizens here in America. It seems like every time Black American citizens experience injustice, we march in the streets fighting to gain liberty and the pursuit of happiness in this great country, but now is the time we should be asking the court system for due process. Because the blood of our ancestors is in the soil of this great country, and we have the right to live with the Statue of Liberty, having the freedom and the opportunities like every other citizen, no matter the skin color. Ever since our ancestors arrived in this country our civil rights have been violated as human being – the Statue of Liberty has a rich meaning not only to White Americans citizen but also to Black and Brown American citizens. It's demonstrate independence from slavery by helping to win the Civil War, because the day after represent the true independence day for Black American citizens. That gave hope to the Negro Christian Slaves, when their chains were broken, and gaves them hope in sharing in the America dream of equal protection of the law.

The United Nations has a primary responsibility for international peace and security: In the Universal Declaration of Human Rights, which brought human rights into the realm of international law, the term "Human Right" is mentioned seven times in the United Nations; founding charter making them the promotion and protection of human rights and this has been a key purpose and guiding principle of the organization since 1948. Also in 1988, President Ronald Reagan – signed the Civil Liberties Act establishing reparations for the victims of Japanese internment into law, while the descendants of the Negro Slaves have not received anything! Ta-Nehisi Coates ignited a conversation for "Reparations" because of slavery and Jim Crow Laws, and what exactly the U.S. Government owes their Black citizens for the unjust treatment and racial disparities. Black American citizen cannot win a case in the America court system for reparations maybe we need to take this issue up in the United Nations. Because they have the responsibility to protect and embody a political commitment to end the worst forms of violence and persecution and seek to narrow a gap between member states pre-existing obligations under international humanitarian and human rights laws. We have to deal with the reality faced by many populations – that is at risk of genocide, war crimes, ethnic cleansing and crimes against humanity.

What Black American citizens need someone to represent us in front of the United Nations, to bring charges against the United States of America – and recommend that they pay African Americans, reparations for the past crimes of hurt and suffering, murder, lynching, rape, Jim Crow, policies, procedures, regulation and redlining that separated the wealth gap between the White and Black citizens. And then we can intervene in the international law for a third-party lawsuit against Spanish and Portugal government for the intentional discrimination to the Black Hebrew Jewish people: The Tribes of Judah, Benjamin and Levi, which got tagged with the name Negro Christian Slave.

Conclusion

We know that reparations can take on many different forms like monetary payment, community investments, improving the education system in the Black and Brown communities, but what history has taught us is that reparations for past harm are possible. However, we cannot let the federal government off the hook, because it going to take at less or around three billion dollars per state to pay Black and Brown citizen reparations. And this is just an approximation to try an eliminate the racial wealth gap. The point of reparations is all about acknowledgment and redress for grievous injustice referring to the perpetrators that committed historic domestic terrorist crimes of human rights. An example of this is when the victims of the Holocaust were paid reparations by both country the U.S. of America and Germany, even though the U.S. was not the perpetrators and also the U.S. paid the Japanese American reparations. But did you know that they paid the Americans hostage who was held in Tehran, Iran. Which got paid reparations back in 1979 around $10,000 per day of captivity so the federal government has set a precedent for paying reparations for atrocities and harms that was committed against U.S. citizens. Te-Nehisi Coates, once quoted "If I injure you; the injury persists even after, I actually commit the act, if I stabbed you; you may suffer complications long after the initial stabbing, this is the case of some African Americans.

The difference between the Black race and other group of people here in America, is that we are the only group of people historical been injustice that never been redressed. If you don't know that ending injustice is not the same thing as redress the enduring side effects of slavery. If we just started in the year of 1776 when America became "Independent" and slavery was still legal to 1860, and added up the enslaved population (x) the hour of worked (x) wages (+) added conservative interest of 3% = we arrived to an outstanding debt over $20 trillion dollars. In this calculation was done by; Thomas Craemer – Ph.D., Political Science, Stony Brook University and Teaching & Research Interests: In race relations and slavery reparations. Professor - Thomas Craemer has used both traditional as well as new methods in survey research to investigate the psychology of race. He used the census information about the enslaved population from each year from 1776 to 1860, or we can say, compound interest. So, this is just one way of proving that reparations are not a handout, but a debt not paid! It's the systemic ways in which African American, have been prevented from building up generational wealth. The psychological trauma part of slavery was not taught in public school or I don't know if this part of Black History, should be talk about? Or when will America ever acknowledge that the psychological damage this country did to the Black race during and after slavery. The grassroots movement for reparations which was led by a Black woman name – Callie House.

Back in the 1890's, Ms. House, made a claim to the federal government for a pension: Ex-Slave Mutual Relief, Bounty & Pension Fund Association of the United States of America. To all local ex-slave associations in the U.S. – we come with greeting, as General Manager and Promoter of the movement. Which had so much opposition and more suppose in its circle than any other organization of their present day. Ms. House used the U.S. Postal Service to communicate with Washington D.C., and to encourage ex-slaved to join the movement, about 300,000 members were paying dues, but the United States Government in response accused her of using the mail system for fraud and was actually convicted by a all-white jury to one year in the federal prison. And if we want to talk about white privilege throughout American history; reparations has been paid out but to the wrong side - the "Slave Owners." The French government sent a fleet to Haiti, to demand reparations for the abolition of slavery there, similarly the British government paid reparations to the enslavers owners in Great Britain, and the United States paid reparations to slave owners in Washington D.C. When slavery was abolished in 1863 and all of the recipients of reparations were white man and white woman, so why do paying reparations only becomes controversial when the recipients are African-Americans? What is HR 40? This bill was introduced in House on 01-03-2019 – Commission to Study and Develop Reparation Proposals for African Americans Act. The commission shall examine slavery and discrimination in the colonies and the United States from 1619 to the present and recommend appropriate remedies.

Among other requirements, the commission shall identify (1) the role of the federal and state government in supporting the institution of slavery, (2) forms of discrimination in the public and private sectors against freed slaves and their descendants, and (3) lingering negative effects of slavery on the living African-Americans also their society. And this was introduced to Congress in 1989 by Rep. John Conyers. The sad thing about slavery that no one wants to talk about is Slave Breeding! Which is often overlooked facet part of America History and Black History. This was the dark side of slavery that nobody wants to talk about and after the United States would potentially cease importation of slaves in the1800's but took effect in 1808, making it illegal to engage in trade between nations but the slaves owners capitalized on breeding of human being like they were livestock. Slavery was already a brutal system for the love of money; now throw in another highly calculated economic system – slave breeding for human capital. However, a domestic or coastwise trade in slaves persisted between ports within the United States, as demonstrated by slave manifests and court records. Let's started with Isaac Franklin (May 26, 1789 – April 27, 1846), he was an American slave trader and plantation owner – also the co-founder of Franklin & Armfield. Which became the largest slave trading firm in the United States, based in Alexandria, Virginia. Mr. Franklin had an offices in New Orleans and other parts of Louisiana and in Tennessee. Overall, he had six plantations but his number one plantation was in Sumner County, Tennessee: And formerly listed on the National Register of Historic Places.

And in the late 19th century, his widow eventually sold the Louisiana plantations in West Feliciana Parish. And his former Angola plantation and other plantations were bought by the state back in 1901, and were converted for use of Louisiana State Penitentiary, the largest maximum-security prison in the United States. Mr. Franklin, business ledgers wasn't filled with crops but with human being, "Black Slaves" each carrying a price tag not only for trading but also for slaves breeding. Because it was cheaper to reproduce a slave then to import one, and the federal law prohibited that no new slaves were permitted by the United States Constitution. This emotional damages got added to the psychological trauma part of Black history, and how the enslaved people were value through their age, health and skill sets. But for the women it was for their fertility making! Their value increased after they were subjected to humiliation by a physical examination to gauge their breeding capabilities. Another slave owner by the name of - Mr. Hinton Rowan Helper, of North Carolina; in 1857 he wrote a book called: The Impending Crisis Of The South: How To Meet It Estimating. The average breeding for an enslave woman could deliver to her owner up to $4,000 dollar worth of property throughout her lifetime. This horrific practice was economically incentivized to capture the economics of slave breeding. The movie 12 Years Of Slavery - shown glimpse of this based on the Memoir of Solomon Northup. The slaves were lineup inspected like they were livestock ready for auction, however the crazy thing about this practice, there were laws in place that sanctioned this act!

The Laws of Virginia Act XII (The Partus Sequitur Ventrem Law) – Negro women children to serve according to the condition of the mother; whereas some doubts have arisen whether children got by any Englishman upon a negro woman should be slave or free. Be it therefore enacted and declared by this present grand assembly that all children born in this country shall be held bond or free only according to the condition of the mother. And that if any Christian shall commit fornication with a negro man or woman, he or she offending shall pay double the fines imposed by the former act. Slave breeding was the dark side of the financial system of slavery, a rule designed to sustain a perpetual labor force (the offspring follows the womb) this colonial law was passed in the 1600's, locking the mother and the child in the system of slavery. The system of slavery was about economics and this law removed the need for fresh body slave, because with this law slave will regenerate itself with fresh new labor force and the plantation owners saw this slave breeding as a win-win to increase their economic. However as of today no one has calculate in the compound interst on this market of slaves breeding for reparation. This law not only divided families but the slave community which added trauma, suffering and mental illness by taking away the children's from their parents. Another law was added called: Jim Crow – these laws enforced racial segregation in the South between the Reconstruction era and the beginning of the Civil Rights Movement, back in the 1950's. This perpetuates systemic of racial inequality lingering the shadow of reminder of hate.

There were auction houses throughout the Southern States from New Orleans to South Carolina, that produce – "Fancy Girl" white men having sex the enslaved woman and sometime the white women having sex with the enslaved man and this was the ultimate commodity but mostly it was the white men. This terminology masked a brutal reality of the mixed race deliberately slave breeding *(in some cases – "Rap")* to produce a lighter skin negro baby was an asset for the slave traders. Prominent names like; Nathan Bedford Forest a notorious slave trader, before his infamous role in the American Civil War. His key role in this market was to trade "Fancy Girls" knowing they could be sold three times the price of a dark skin enslaved women. And advertised them by emphasizing on their youth and beauty but not only these women were physically violated also they were reduced to objects. Harriet Jacobs, who wrote the autobiography; Incident in The Life of a Slave Girl – gives a harrowing account of the degradation and the psychological torment suffered by the negro women. The 2013 film called: BELLE – touched upon the complexities of this objectification in a British context, and there is another book called: Celia A Slave. By: Melton A. McLaurin. Presents a gut-wrenching tale of a "Fancy Girl" revealing the pain and humiliation these women went through. Now, there are equally disturbing aspect of the dark side of slave breeding, which is called: "Stub Services." The dehumanization of enslaved men and enslaved women. The male slaves were rendered not as fathers, husbands or brothers but "Studs" hired out for their reproductive abilities.

No difference then livestock or any other animal making the male enslaved with certain desired traits were often rented out to other plantation owners and were documented in various estate inventories in the farm journals as human being's property assets. This horrifying example can be found in the ledger books of Zephaniah Kingsley Jr. and the Atlantic World: Slave Trader, Plantation Owner Emancipator, by Daniel L. Schafer. He was a plantation owner in Florida - that had a transaction record for renting out male slaves as stubs services. This was rooted as the racist science of eugenics belief that specific added to the physical and the mental damages in the Black race. Enslaved breeding led to the economic incentives for the plantation owners, hoping that selective breeding may build the next generation of enslaved people to be stronger and healthier therefore may led up to be more profitable. This made the enslaved woman take their reproduction system in their own hands, living in the outrageous conditions of the plantation owners they started to resistance this kind of reproductive system. Which force them to have babies for their owner making profits off of human life. The women intentionally employed covert methods like herbal medicines to prevent pregnancy quietly fighting back against slave breeding. Harriet Tubman and Sojourner Truth helped to empower the enslaved women and men to preservation their family. But the discovery meant severe punishment or death these emotional narratives of our passed history are stories of strength and resilience amidst out of the darkness part of slavery.

The economic considerations that drove this brutal system that torn families apart were pure evil, leaving deep emotional scars that lasting all the way up to today's generation well into the 21st century. We see evidence of scars in the Black community when it comes down to families. Back then the Black families were deliberately torn apart from their families - mothers, fathers, brothers and sisters. They were reduced to commodities, sold to the highest bidder with no regard for their emotional and psychological trauma. We have movies like "Roots" that give us a glimpse of the life of enslaved people. But we cannot imagine their trauma and what they were thinking or their repercussions of losing family members, or being in their place especially in the context of slave breeding. The narratives that come out of Hollywood underscore the real anguish and trauma that was inflicted on the enslaved people. The evil perpetuated cycle of suffering for years, can we really imagine the pain. The White slave owner even enforced religious for justification on the enslaved people to a disturbing aspect twisted manipulation to reinforce obedience to their master by using the Holy Bible - that they put together. Already converted into Christianity not knowing the contents of their new religion; they were given a book that was distorted to justify the horrors of slave breeding. They selectively cherry-picked scriptures to support their motive of servitude and overlooking other scriptures like; compassion, justice and liberation. But they endorsed slavery like: Ephesians 6:5-8 that says, "Slaves, obey your earthly masters with respect and fear, and with sincerity of heart, just as you would obey Christ.

223

Obey them not only to win their favor when their eye is on you, but like slaves of Christ, doing the will of God from your heart. Serve wholeheartedly, as if you were serving the Lord, not men, because you know that the Lord will reward everyone for whatever good he does, whether he is slave or free." What kind of evil person would take advantage of another human being which didn't speak their language? Slavery was terrible for a Black man, but it was far more terrible for a Black woman! The truth is all around us, about who we are, and who we are not! It's hidden in plain sight, so the best way for me to end this book is by asking each of you to watch these documentaries starting with: Reclaiming the Throne – this is a three part documentary so *(Please; used your Fire Stick or Netflix or Tubi, to search for this document)*. They will take you on a detailed dive into biblical prophecies as well historical and scientific research about the children of Israel's identity. Hopefully, these documentaries will answer many questions about the true identity of African Americans and empower the Black communities to see themselves in history by uncovering and revealed the truth color of our Messiah. And let the necessity of facts rule your decision about His historical physical characteristic skin color. And His real name. Also let His ontological show the relations between the concepts and categories in a subject area or domain branching of metaphysics dealing with the nature of His being. No matter how hard we try to disconnect Him from His ethnicity, which is – Hebrew. We shouldn't!

The world has to accept all of Him, or nothing at all! Because the world doesn't have the luxury to say: We are going to confirm His ethnicity and His name to be – Jesus Christ, because this is - Imperialism. Now is the time to "Wake Up" because the fulfillment of the Gentiles is almost complete. I'm not crying wolf, or do I dare to try, but we're standing at the crossroad of making a decision – Tradition vs. Scripture. And a decision has to be made, we cannot continue to say asleep because the Messiah will come like a thief in the night. Our; Former President Donald Trump - once said: To the African American communities in his first campaign – "What do you have to lose" but I am sorry to say: If we do not wake up, our "Salvation" is at stake.

Psalm 151

This Psalm is ascribed to David as his own composition though it is outside the number, after he had fought in a single combat with Goliath: According to ETH CEPHER in Psalms 151 that says, "I WAS the youngest among my brethren and a youth in my father's house. I used to feed my father's flock and I found a lion and a wolf and slew them and rent them. My hands made a flute and my fingers fashioned a harp. Who will show me my **Adonai**? He, my **Adonai**, is become my **Elohiym**. He sent his Angel and took me away from my father's flock and anointed me with the oil of anointing. My brethren, the fair and the tall, in them **Yahuah** had no pleasure. And I went forth to meet the Pelishtiy, and he cursed me by his idols. But I drew his sword and cut off his head, and took away the reproach from the children of Yashar'el (Israel)."

But I drew his *(own)* sword; and cut off his head and took away the reproach from the children of Yashar'el *(Israel)*." King David – was a Black man over the House of Israel and when the Messiah come for His Sabbath Rest on Earth for One Thousand Years: He will be a Black Man, over the Kingdom of God. We cannot afford to forget: Who we are! Slavery was more than 400 hundred years but 1,000 years: Please watch this documentary on the YouTube channel: 1,000 years a Slave – History Document. To get a better understanding of how God's, scattered his people to the four corners of the world. According to the NIV Quiet Time Bible in Isaiah 11:10-16 that says, "In that day the Root of Jesse will stand as a banner for the peoples the nations will rally to him, and his place of rest will be glorious. In that day, the Lord will reach out his hand a second time to reclaim the remnant that is left of his people from Assyria, from Lower Egypt, from Upper Egypt, from Cush, from Elam, from Babylonia, from Hamath and from the islands of the sea. He will raise a banner for the nations and gather the exiles of Israel: He will assemble the scattered people of Judah from the four quarters of the earth. Ephraim will not be jealous of Judah, nor Judah hostile toward Ephraim. They will swoop down on the slopes of Philistia to the west; together they will plunder the people to the east. They will lay hands on Edom and Moab, and the Ammonites will be subject to them. The LORD will dry up the gulf of the Egyptian sea; with a scorching wind He will sweep his hand over the Euphrates River. He will break it up into seven streams so that men can cross over in sandals.

There will be a highway for the remnant of his people that is left from Assyria, as there was for Israel: When they came up from Egypt." Amein.

About the Author

While some leaders are created, others are born to lead. As an agent of change, author and soldier—spiritually and naturally leader —Wallace Stanciel knows firsthand how to weather times of war and come out victorious on the other side. As a United States Army veteran retiree and retired from the United States Postal Service. Mr. Stanciel prides himself on being a man of discipline, values and integrity. And while he loves personally winning and enjoying life, his greatest passion and pursuit is to see the people whom he loves growing and living a life of fulfillment. Recognizing that the Black race is a forgiving race: Wallace Stanciel seeks to open blinded eyes to the unadulterated truth about the identity of "Who we are" as the Black race as a whole.

Intentional about living a long life, Wallace, loves sports, fitness and healthy eating lifestyle. Realizing that two of life's most precious assets is time, and relationships with friends and family. He is a mighty man of valor whether he's on the battlefield literally or figuratively, God always come first! Understanding that the Black race has achieved everything they we were striving for, he believes the race as a whole is at the crossroad of the valley of decisions. Tradition versus Scripture, is where this road gets narrow. And he's more than qualified to lead others down the right road.

Holding both an Associate's and a Bachelor's degree in Business Administration Specializing in Human Resource Management from Davenport University. Wallace also holds an MBA in Business Administration from the University of Phoenix, Specializing in Operational Management. In addition, he attended Capella University's in there three years Accelerated Doctoral degree program in Business Administration Specializing in Innovation and Stratetgy but was unable to finish due to medical issues. In his debut book, Wallace takes readers on a journey of self-discovery—not just of themselves—but of the Black race as a whole. Intentional about educating and empowering Black people to stop living a life of destruction, he singlehandedly peels back the layers that cause Black people to intentionally hurt one another because of our mental condition surrounding slavery and racial disparities. He does this through encouraging the Black race to become - Self-Autonomous: Ushering oursleves to become more empower and moral independence of finding the truth about who we are! And what is behind this religion we have been worshipped for decades.

For booking or speaking engagements, email wallacestanciel61@yahoo.com.

References

Padgett, Alan G. (1992). God, Eternity and the Nature of Time, London: Macmillan. (Reprint, Wipf and Stock, 2000.

Padgett, Alan G. (2001). Eternity as Relative Timelessness, in Ganssle (2001a): 92-110.

Craig, William Lane and Quentin Smith. (1993). Theism, Atheism, and Big Bang Cosmology. Oxford: Oxford University Press.

Craig, William Lane. (2001b). Timelessness and Omnitemporality, in Ganssle (2001a): 129-160.

Craig, William Lane. (2002). The Elimination of Absolute Time by the Special theory of Relativity, in Ganssle and Woodruff (2002): 129-152.

DeWeese, Garrett J. (2002). Atemporal, Sempiternal or Omintemporal: God's Temporal Mode of Being, in Ganssle and Woodruff (2002a): 49-61

DeWeese, Garrett J. (2004). God and the Nature of Time. Hampshire UK: Ashgate.

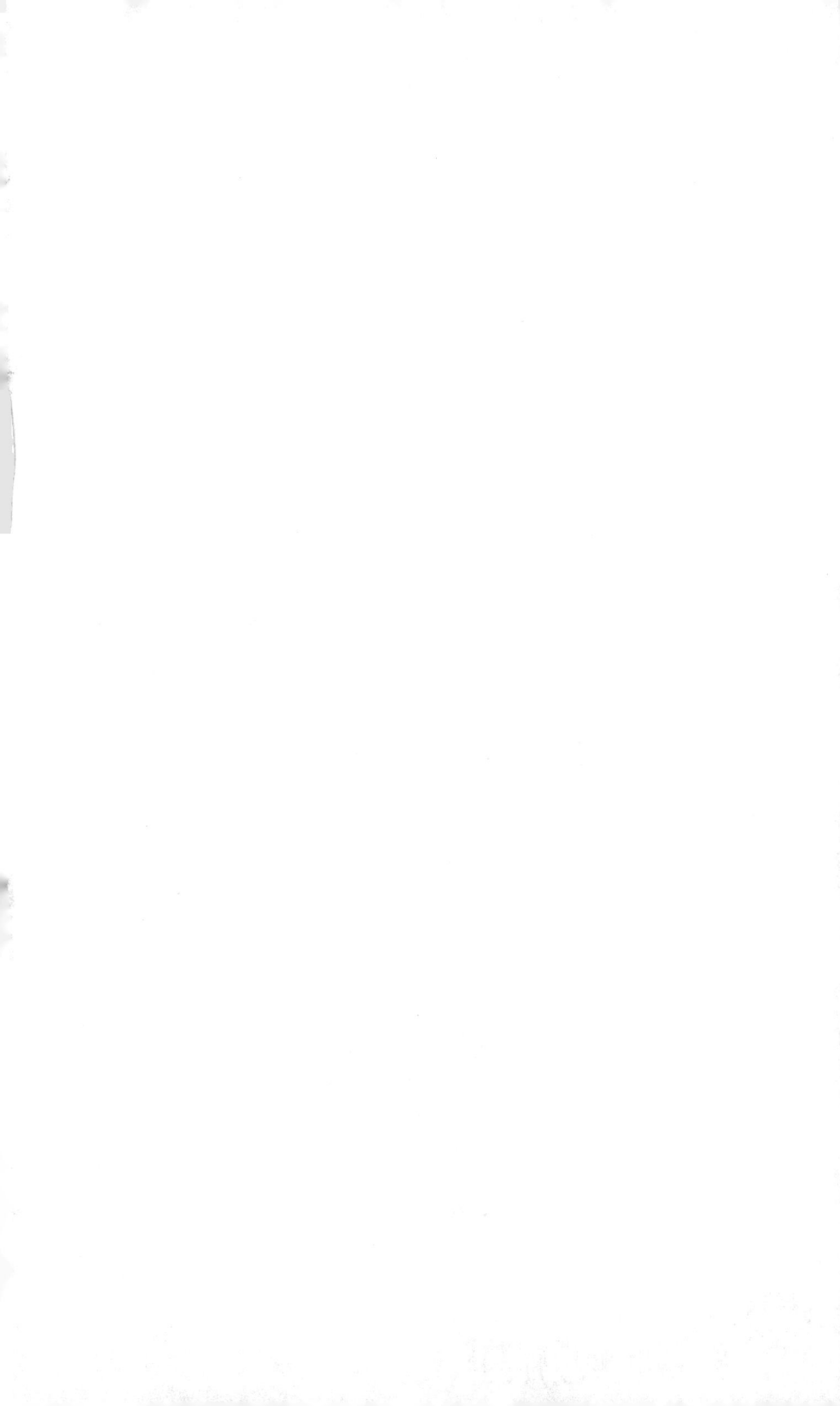